PIERCING THE DARKNESS

THROUGH SPIRITUAL WARFARE
AND DELIVERANCE

DR LARRY RECK

BALBOA.
PRESS

A DIVISION OF HAY HOUSE

Scripture taken from the *Amplified Bible*, Copyright © 1954, 1958, 1962, 1964, 1965, 1987 by The Lockman Foundation. Used by permission.

Dake's Annotated Reference Bible. Dake Publishing, Inc. 764 Martins Chapel Rd. Lawrenceville, GA, 30045. www. info@dake.com. 1963.

Scripture taken from The Living Bible copyright © 1971 by Tyndale House Foundation. Used by permission of Tyndale House Publishers Inc., Carol Stream, Illinois 60188. All rights reserved. The Living Bible, TLB, and the The Living Bible logo are registered trademarks of Tyndale House Publishers.

Scriptures taken from the Holy Bible, New International Version®, NIV®. Copyright © 1973, 1978, 1984, 2011 by Biblica, Inc.™ Used by permission of Zondervan. All rights reserved worldwide. www.zondervan.com The "NIV" and "New International Version" are trademarks registered in the United States Patent and Trademark Office by Biblica, Inc.™ All rights reserved.

Balboa Press books may be ordered through booksellers or by contacting:

Balboa Press
A Division of Hay House
1663 Liberty Drive
Bloomington, IN 47403
www.balboapress.com
1 (877) 407-4847

Because of the dynamic nature of the Internet, any web addresses or links contained in this book may have changed since publication and may no longer be valid. The views expressed in this work are solely those of the author and do not necessarily reflect the views of the publisher, and the publisher hereby disclaims any responsibility for them.

The author of this book does not dispense medical advice or prescribe the use of any technique as a form of treatment for physical, emotional, or medical problems without the advice of a physician, either directly or indirectly. The intent of the author is only to offer information of a general nature to help you in your quest for emotional and spiritual well-being. In the event you use any of the information in this book for yourself, which is your constitutional right, the author and the publisher assume no responsibility for your actions.

Any people depicted in stock imagery provided by Thinkstock are models, and such images are being used for illustrative purposes only. Certain stock imagery © Thinkstock.

Printed in the United States of America.

ISBN: 978-1-4525-2179-4 (sc)
ISBN: 978-1-4525-2180-0 (e)

Balboa Press rev. date: 09/04/2014

CONTENTS

This book is dedicated to my loving and faithful wife, Sheri who was instrumental in encouraging me to put my experiences in print and to delineate those things that are happening in the secular and spiritual world of which many people are unaware. She is also a member of "God's Squad" or the deliverance team. We pray that this book will help you in both your secular and spiritual walk in life and how to overcome many of the problems of a spiritual nature that we all encounter.

INTRODUCTION

I want to thank you for choosing this book to help increase your knowledge of spiritual warfare and deliverance. Hopefully, it will prepare you in your battle against the dark forces of this world – how to identify them, deal with them and how to remove them. This book is a compilation of knowledge and experience of over one-hundred years of four persons working together in a team.

The first member of "God's Squad" as my precious wife Sheri calls us, whom I married in 2008, has added experiences of her own in this book. She is a talented musician and soloist and in demand for her song writing and playing ability. As a child, she was declared dead in a Tennessee hospital for thirty-eight minutes at which time she walked hand-in-hand with Jesus as He showed her heaven and the future new Jerusalem where a single pearl makes up each of the gates. The streets literally are gold and the water is so clear that she could see her reflection in it. She wanted to stay but Jesus said she must go back and minister to others. Sheri has a strong gift of Discernment. Sheri's mom, Wilma Lee Payne has also been supportive in my teaching and ministry and has given me much encouragement in writing this book.

Pastor Marion (Bud) Hoard has been a minister and pastor for many years and operates in all of the gifts of the Holy Spirit. Some examples are contained within this book. He is a very valued member of the team.

Pastor Joe Green is another valued member of the team. His prayers, primarily when ministering in pre-deliverance and post-deliverance are anointed and inspired. Some of the examples in this book are from his experiences. Joe went to Russia on four evangelistic out-reaches. Two were with me as we ministered to thousands of people.

Information regarding my life and experiences are located later in this Introduction. I was a pastor for seven years and at the time of this writing still do pulpit supply in various denominational churches. I have given numerous teachings on spiritual warfare, deliverance, satanism, occult, cults, demonology and other "dark-side" topics. After giving over eight-hundred teachings on these topics, I have since lost count but the deliverance team is still active in teaching and ministry. Examples contained in this book are from my experiences and also those of the combined team.

Bud, Joe and I went to Russia on ministry tours with Revival Fires Ministry under the direction of Dr. Cecil Todd located in Branson West, MO. I had the pleasure of going there three times and ministering to many people in the elementary, secondary, trade school and college levels along with meetings every evening in packed auditoriums. A highlight was participating in ministry at a military base in Moscow (the equivalent of our West Point). Dr. Todd was the speaker. When he gave the altar call, seventy percent of the future officers came forward to receive Jesus and obtain *Russian Bibles*. We were the first Americans ever on that base. It was reassuring to see the American and Russian flags at equal heights for that day in the auditorium. During the three trips we passed out 100,000 Bibles. On one trip I spoke to 1,400 people. People in Russia are very hungry for the Word. The three cities in which I ministered were Ryazan, Moscow and Saratov. My visits to the Kremlin and St. Basil's on Red Square were awesome. I have also taken trips to five European countries and Israel.

I wish to thank my personal physician, Dr. Richard Butler from Union Hospital in Terre Haute, IN for encouraging me to put my experiences down in book form and for his support along the way. He definitely was a help and inspiration to me in this writing. He not only is a great doctor but also a great advisor.

I also want to thank Dr. Tim Mech, professor at Grove City College, PA for providing excellent spiritual insight into the contents of this book. He is a talented writer and was instrumental in editing and refining it along with suggesting new areas of inclusion so as to enhance its understanding and outreach. I appreciate his aid in helping me to reorganize the chapters and content and the removal of repetition to make it more readable. He indeed, was a major contributor to this book.

The purpose of this book is to inform you about the tactics of Satan and the problems he can cause Christians; also, how to identify his influence and what to do about it. Some of the content deals with deliverance and how to remove demons that are oppressing and/or possessing people. A major portion covers how to remain "clean" and our authority we have over all demons in the name of Jesus. A chapter on satanism also is included. The Contents list specifically what is included in this book. I have delineated new content areas in the text with free-standing side-heads.

The result of deliverance is not only to have the demons leave but the change in behavior of that person after deliverance. The proof is from ungodliness to godliness and seeing the person leading a life in Christ without the harassment of Satan. The person now knows how to bind Satan and the demons and how to walk in his or her deliverance.

Names and places used in this book are fictitious to protect individuals and locations, although the names of the deliverance team often appear and are the "actual" people. Events and happenings along with results are all documented and have occurred over a period of time, most within the past two decades. One caveat is that we cannot ascribe all of our short-comings and problems to Satan. We bring on many of these by our own lifestyle and the decisions we make. Life is made up primarily of choices and if we don't include the Lord in them we are heading into disaster.

Read this book with anticipation and with an open heart and mind and may the Lord use it to minister to you. May God grant you love and peace in the name of our Lord and Savior, Jesus Christ who is the same yesterday, and today, and forever (Hebrews 13:8). Romans 2:10 (KJV) lets us know what will happen when we work for Him; "But glory, honor, and peace, to every man that worketh good…"

My Definition Of Spiritual Warfare

Spiritual warfare is the physical, mental, emotional and spiritual preparation to combat Satan's devices that he uses against us. It is preparation to resist every attack of the enemy - as a soldier does in battle. It is our constant struggle against the powers of darkness and with the enemies who would keep us from God and heaven; also, it is putting on the whole armor of God with the defenses and weaponry He has given us for the purpose of repelling the temptations and the stratagems of Satan. Jesus was crucified at a place called Golgotha or the place of the skull. To defeat Satan we must be crucified in the "place of our skull" and be renewed in the spirit of our mind by the Holy Spirit. Briefly, it is putting aside the deeds of darkness and putting on the armor of light. (Ephesians 6:13-18).

MY BIO

Due to the prompting of my wife Sheri and Dr. Richard Butler, I have included a bio section of this book to familiarize you with my background. One of the major reasons for this is that many of the examples contained within may seem bazaar but by sharing my life's experiences, maybe it will help you to know "where I'm coming from" on both the secular and spiritual levels.

My father's family came from Schleswig-Holstein, a state in Northwest Germany. My dad, Carl Henry Reck was born in Racine, WI. and was a carpenter by trade. He made sure we attended church every Sunday and went to Sunday School.

My mother's family came from Germany but moved to Russia on request of the Russian Czar who wanted the German people to help his people farm. One day in 1911, my grandfather was approached by an angel warning him to leave Russia, so the family left and sailed to America. All of my other relatives in Russia died during a forced march to Siberia during the Bolshevik Revolution.

My mother (Ida Platzke) was nine years old when she left Russia with her family. She and my dad had two children. Carl, Jr. was an elementary school principal in Racine, WI. Both parents were devote Christians, never missing a church service, and making sure we were baptized and confirmed. I had a wonderful childhood with loving parents.

I was born in Kenosha, WI. After attending elementary school, I spent my junior high school years at Frieden's Lutheran School. From there it was Kenosha High School where I was involved in the wrestling and baseball programs and the band. I played semi-pro ball and tried out for the majors but didn't make it, so I decided to go to college. I loved learning so much that I could have become a "professional" college student.

While in Kenosha, I was a member of the Wisconsin National Guard, Battery "A" 126 Field Artillery for eight years where as a Staff Sargent I was Chief of Firing Battery with 105mm howitzers. In 1961 I received an honorable discharge from the army.

In 1956 I entered Wisconsin State University-Whitewater where I received a Bachelor of Education degree with six minors: language arts, social studies, fine arts, science, geography and history. I also was selected to "Who's Who in American Colleges and Universities." I taught elementary school in Darien, WI, then moved to Kenosha where I taught science at McKinley JHS and where I met my wife Alice, who passed away in 2002.

Next, I went to the University of Wisconsin where I received a Master of Science in Education degree. I was an assistant while attending during summers. After that I taught at the University of Hawaii where I also was Supervisor of the Instructional Materials Center.

Returning to the mainland, I taught at Wisconsin State University-Eau Claire where I was the director of audio-visual services. From there I went to Indiana State University in Terre Haute for thirty-three years, retiring in 2001. During that time I received my Master of Library Science degree from Indiana University and then my third master's degree (Master of Arts in Religion) from Trinity Evangelical Divinity School in Deerfield, IL. I then received a Doctor of Education degree from the University of New Mexico where I also taught for two years.

To work my way through much of my education I took on a variety of jobs, as truck driver for Standard Oil, Milwaukee Road railroad section hand, car wash attendant, A&P food store worker, school bus driver, pastor – just to name a few.

While at Indiana State University I was advisor to Campus Christian Ministry try for nineteen years. I taught a total of eleven different courses from the undergraduate level to the doctoral program. My areas of expertise were curriculum and instruction, media technology (classroom use of media and computers) and library science. During my final three years at ISU most of my courses were distant education including students from many foreign countries.

One of my greatest honors was when Jeff and Bre Davis named their son Nolan <u>Reck</u> Davis after me. Hopefully he will strive to be a great athlete but more so, a great Christian. He has been a bright light in my life.

I preached and ministered in a Lutheran church for seven years and as I studied the *Bible*, the Lord began to lead me to an area that I had never explored or even had an interest – deliverance. He was dealing with me for six months but I told no one. Then one Sunday we went to hear a guest minister speak, Pastor Bud Hoard. During his message he stopped and pointed to me saying, "The Lord has been dealing with you for six months to get into deliverance. He will protect you physically, mentally, spiritually and provide places for you to speak and minister." Who could deny that, so because of Pastor Bud, I became involved in spiritual warfare and deliverance with the Lord opening many doors for me to preach, teach and minister.

I have read the *Satanic Bible* and many other "dark side" books. The Lord has protected my mind so these have no influence over me. My reason is that I need to know from their own materials what they are doing and not get the information second hand. I study the "dark side" materials so I can be accurate in what I teach and what I write in this book. Of course my major program of study is the *Holy Bible* that I read and study daily.

The experiences you read in this book may seem "far out" and too dark to be true, but after thirty-five years teaching about spiritual warfare, deliverance, cults, occult, demonology, satanism and other dark areas, I feel that I am led by the Lord and qualified to expose these areas to you.

May the Lord open your mind to what is happening in both the secular and and spiritual world as you read this book. Even if you never do any deliverance may it lead you to have the foreknowledge of what to do when bad things start to happen. Hopefully, it will give examples to which you can relate and provide you with guidance and direction in all of your endeavors.

CHAPTER ONE

Establishing The Biblical Foundation

All Scriptures are from the KJV of the Bible except where otherwise noted.

Why did Jesus come to earth? You might say to bring us salvation, hope, peace, love and have life to the fullest which is all correct, but 1 John 3:8 takes it one step further when it says, "For this purpose the Son of God was manifested, that he might *destroy the works of the devil.*"

The *Bible* teaches that Satan and demons exist and that they will attempt to create trouble for Christians. This is an important warning that we would be wise to heed. The story of the Fall in Genesis describes Satan's modus operandi. Satan persuades people that God's prohibitions are unnecessary, that God is merely trying to withhold something good from us. If people accept what Satan is saying, they will distrust and disobey God and be increasingly influenced by Satan.

Everyday temptations and sins parallel the Genesis account. In all of these common temptations, people willfully disobey God, doubting the wisdom or goodness of His commands. This puts them more and more under the influence of evil. Further discussion of these concepts can be found in the chapters to follow.

In Hosea 4:6 we read "My people are destroyed from lack of knowledge." This is what I feel is the basic premise of why many of God's people are struggling in both their spiritual and secular lives. An old adage says an evil thought passes through your door first as a stranger – then it enters as a guest. At the time of this writing, the divorce rate is the same for Christians as for non-Christians. Why are some Christians on drugs, unwed Christians having babies, Christians who are dependent on alcohol, unwed Christians living together as man and wife and Christians having all sorts of problems? Could it be because Satan has a hand in these matters? Could it be that he's enticing these people to do his will? Hopefully this book can help you decide.

What The Bible Says

I want to take you on a biblical excursion with a topic called spiritual warfare. It's about Satan, but mainly our authority over him and how we can control his influence in our lives and remove, or at least alleviate many of our problems; but first, let's look at what Revelation 12:7-13 and verse 17 have to say:

"And there was war in heaven. Michael and his angels fought against the dragon, and the dragon and his angels fought back. But he was not strong enough, and they lost their place in heaven. The great dragon was hurled down — that ancient serpent called the devil, or Satan, who leads the whole world astray. He was hurled to the earth, and his angels with him. Then I heard a loud voice in heaven say: "Now have come the salvation and the power and the kingdom of our God, and the authority of his Christ. For the accuser of our brothers, who accuses them before our God day and night has been hurled down. They overcame him by the blood of the Lamb and by the word of their testimony; they did not love their lives so much as to shrink from death. Therefore rejoice, you heavens and you who dwell in them! But woe to the earth and the sea, because the devil has gone down to you! He is filled with fury, because he knows that his time is short." (Verse 17) "Then the dragon was enraged at the woman and went off to make war against the rest of her offspring — those who obey God's commandments and hold to the testimony of Jesus."

Do we as Christians obey God's Commandments and hold the testimony of Jesus? Then are we the ones that Satan is after? He already has the non- Christians so now he is after us! According to Matthew 4, Jesus was tempted by Satan but

Jesus told him in verses 4,7 and 10: "It is written…" Outside of the name of Jesus, these are the most powerful words you can use in spiritual warfare. I will expound further on these words in the following chapters. If Jesus was tempted, how much more can Satan tempt us?

Other Biblical Persons Tempted By Satan

Look what happened to Job in 1:8: "Then the Lord said to Satan, Have you considered my servant Job? There is no one on earth like him; he is blameless and upright, a man who fears God and shuns evil." If this was the character of Job and he was tempted, can Satan get to us?

Beware! In 2 Timothy 2:24-26 Paul is talking to Christians saying "And the Lord's servant must not quarrel; instead, he must be kind to everyone, able to teach, not resentful. Those who oppose him he must gently instruct, in the hope that God will grant them repentance leading them to a knowledge of the truth, and that they will come to their senses and escape from the trap of the devil, *who has taken them captive to do his will.*" In 1 Corinthians 5:1 a believer had problems. "It is actually reported that there is sexual immorality among you, and of a kind that does not occur even among pagans: a man has his father's wife."

Even one of Jesus' disciples was tempted. We read the following in John 13:26b-27: "Then, dipping the piece of bread, He (Jesus) gave it to Judas Iscariot, son of Simon. As soon as Judas took the bread, Satan entered into him."

Did Paul always have peace? Let's see what he said in 2 Corinthians 12:7: "To keep me from becoming conceited because of these surpassingly great revelations, there was given me a thorn in my flesh, *a messenger of Satan*, to torment me."

CHAPTER TWO

Weaknesses That Open Us Up To Satan

I have often heard when someone starts to read the *Bible* that he or she becomes extremely tired. They can be very perky when they begin but suddenly they become too tired to continue. Most likely Satan is at work here. Another attack is when you have uncontrollable urges and temptations or continuous negative feelings which are overwhelming and reoccurring. It might be an obsession or compulsive behavior which is almost impossible to overcome without the help of Jesus.

How Satan And His Demons Work

In my thirty-five years of teaching spiritual warfare and doing numerous deliverances, I have found many who were demon oppressed or demonized, but few who were totally possessed. There will be much more on this in later chapters.

When we open our door to Satan and his demons they will enter. If we keep feeding them with our thoughts and actions they will certainly oppress us. How many times would you go back to an empty refrigerator? If there is nothing to feed them, they will not come back. The idea is to always keep your refrigerator clean!

One deliverance team member, Joe Green compares a person's heart to a hotel. Our heart is made up of many rooms, most of them we keep swept out but there are a few in which we keep the doors locked – our secret sins – secret to people but known by the demons. These rooms are where we are attacked. If we do not keep all of the rooms clean we will have problems. Remember, Satan cannot read are minds since he's only a fallen angel but our actions give us away. He always seems to be there to entice us when we go astray.

Enslavement

Be careful about enslavement to temptations as certain heavy metal music or excessive television viewing where breaking away is difficult to overcome. Another attack by Satan is fear. I knew a high school boy that stayed awake all night because he was afraid that "ghosts" would come into his room. I had him read Psalm 34:4, "I sought the Lord, and he heard me, and delivered me from *all my fears.*"

Unforgiveness

The number one problem that my deliverance team and I have found is unforgiveness. This seems to be bother-some for many Christians to forgive. Let's look at some Scriptures that bring this out. Isaiah 59:2 is very succinct in saying "Your iniquities have separated you from your God; your sins have hidden his face from you, *so that he will not hear.*" In Matthew 18:35 we read, "This is how my heavenly Father will treat each of you *unless you forgive* your brother from your heart."

I believe Mark 11:26 is the crux of unforgiveness. "If ye do not forgive, neither will your Father which is in heaven forgive your trespasses." John 9:31 sums this up by saying, "We know that *God does not listen to sinners.* He listens to the godly man who does his will."

My team has ministered to many divorced persons. We have asked each person these two questions: (1) have you forgiven your former spouse and (2) does God answer your prayers? One hundred percent of those who had not forgiven stated that God *does not* hear my prayers. Many stated it's like trying to get through a concrete ceiling. One-hundred percent of those persons who had forgiven said yes, God *does* answer my prayers. What amazing statistics! I believe these percentages speak for themselves. If you do not forgive, you are a sinner and God does not hear your prayers, but if you forgive, God's ears are open to your requests. There's an old proverb that states, "He who cannot forgive others, breaks the bridge over which he, himself, must pass."

Delving Into The Dark Areas

When we delve into areas as astrology, palm reading, the occult, horoscopes, fortune telling, séances, witchcraft, covens and rituals, divination, tarot card reading, channeling, black magick (magic), Wicca, spells, charms, earth religions, spiritualism, soul travel (astral projection), automatic writing and other dark areas we play into the hands of Satan. How far can Satan push us? As far as we let him, and often-times we don't even realize what's happening until it's too late. By living a clean life we should know when Satan is about to strike. We need to keep Jesus central in our lives and in control of our thoughts, words and deeds; then Satan will be kept at bay. Paul gives us some practical advice in 1 Corinthians 10: 20b-21: "... I do not want you to be participants with demons. You cannot drink the cup of the Lord and the cup of demons too; you cannot have a part in both the Lord's table and the table of demons." We cannot serve two masters.

Law Of Generations

You probably have heard the phrase, "like father like son." This is what is known as "The Law of Generations." One day one of my team members, Pastor Bud Hoard, called me to help minister to a young lady. Her mother had arthritis so badly that she was bend over and could barely move. The day she died, her oldest daughter became so arthritic she could hardly move. The day the oldest daughter died, this youngest daughter became so arthritic that she had great difficulty in moving. When we took her through an hour of deliverance she was completely set free and at this writing still remains free. Here is an example of how demons can use the Law of Generations against us. Binding in the name of Jesus (as described in future chapters) can be one of the major ways to handle spiritual problems.

The *Bible* brings out this law in a number of places. In Deuteronomy 28:5 we find the warning that "The Lord will send fearful plagues on you and your descendants, harsh and prolonged disasters, and severe and lingering illnesses." Nehemiah 9:2 says "Those of Israelite descent had separated themselves from all foreigners. They stood in their places and confessed their sins and the wickedness *of their fathers*." Why did they confess what their fathers did? This was to guarantee that their sins and transgressions would not be passed down to future generations.

Exodus 20:5-6 expounds on this in further detail. "I, the Lord your God, am a jealous God, *punishing the children for the sin of the fathers* to the third and fourth generation of those who hate me, but showing love to a thousand generations of those who love me and keep my commandments." Finally in Lamentations 5:7 we read that "Our fathers sinned and are no more, and *we bear their punishment*."

Excessive Restlessness

Restlessness is another way in which I have noted demonic activity. An example of this is when I was speaking in a church, every time I said the name "Jesus" a young man would just quiver and shake uncontrollably. After the service when most of the people had departed, I called him up and asked what happened when I mentioned Jesus. He said he was the youth minister at that church and to demonstrate to his youth how it felt to have demons in them, he asked the demons to possess him but now he could not get them out . After I commanded the demons to come out in the name of Jesus he was set free. He willfully opened himself up to be taken over by Satan. Life is a series of choices but this one was probably the worst I have ever encountered, and of all people – a minister.

If you constantly feel sick, tired or weak, dirty, unclean or defiled it *may* (and I emphasize *may*) be a demonic attack. Care must be taken, for not every problem is an attack by Satan. We bring many problems on ourselves by poor decisions and erroneous choices as exemplified by that youth minister. Ask God to help you make your decisions.

Certain multiple personality disorders could possibly be an attack. Many times when young children are sexually molested they develop another personality as a survival technique. One of the team members, Joe Green, encountered a young lady that had taken on nineteen personalities. He and another minister had to approach each personality before she was set free.

Negative Feelings

Also, you may be attacked if you have a group of similar feelings such as (a) suicide, rebellion, destruction, death, (b) rejection, bitterness, rebellion, (c) worry, anxiety, dread, fear, apprehension, and (d) self-accusation, self-hatred or self-condemnation. Another aspect to watch is any history of the occult in the paternal and maternal backgrounds. One girl indicated that she had witch-like feelings that were difficult to control. She stated her aunt was a witch. These tendencies were passed down to her.

Be aware if your love of Jesus and reading the Word are getting cold. Don't bank on your past laurels. Remember, Lucifer was once in heaven. Solomon wrote many psalms and proverbs but when he turned from the Lord what did he say in Ecclesiastes 1:2? "Vanity of vanities, saith the Preacher, vanity of vanities; all is vanity." Remember the best deliverance is to live a clean life, fast, pray and study the Word.

Not Knowing The Word Of God

You can be attacked if you do not know the Word of God. Your mind is in the middle; God is on one side – Satan on the other. Now whom will you let control your mind? If you don't choose God, Satan will automatically move in. You must be aware of Satan's devices. Pew research brings out that the average Christian spends only three and one-half minutes per day in prayer. The order in which I teach prayer is (1) praise God for His love and grace to you and for who He is, (2) thank Him for your blessings, (3) ask for forgiveness and repent so nothing stands between you and Him, (4) pray for others, (5) pray for your needs, and lastly (6) *listen* to what He has to say to you. This last step produces many downfalls in our prayer life when we don't give Him time to talk to us.

So often we are so busy that we take our eyes off of Jesus and onto our own problems. Dwell on the Lord from whom all blessings flow. Are you aware of Satan's devices? If not, why not? Are you not getting into the Word? Don't just read the *Bible, study* it!

Using The Quiji Board

You can easily be attacked if you play with the quiji board. This is one of the most common entrances into the demonic world that one can pursue. One lady told me that three times she threw her board into the trash but the next day it was back. A women on a television program said she tore her board into small pieces but the next day it was back on her shelf in one piece. Is Satan at work here?

Another lady said she went to a slumber party as a teen-ager. The board told her she would die on her birthday. For thirty-five years she lived in fear as to which birthday it would be. I heard of a boy who played with the board. It told him that he will die that day before the sun goes down. He went to both his dad and minister. Apparently neither knew the power of the board so they told him to simply forget about it. Before nightfall, the boy took his dad's gun and killed himself. Oh, the power of suggestion of the board. One of my former neighbors (who since has moved to another state) called me and said that there were seven green "ghosts" flouting around in her home, also being seen by seven college students who were visiting. She said they were the spirits of the "restless dead." I asked her if she had a quiji board in her house. She said they had just been playing with it. I questioned her if she ever asked where its power came from. She said, "yes, it said from Satan." I asked if that frightened her. Her response: "it's only a game." Oh, how misled can one be when playing in Satan's realm. I took her board and started to burn it. Horrendous screeches came from it. I called my wife to come outside to listen so I'd have proof of what was happening. As she approached the board, the birds in the area made such a loud noise that they drowned out the screeches. This happened twice before I finally destroyed it. A friend of mine had a similar experience. As he was burning a board the flames jumped up toward him and singed the front of his body.

One day a Christian father called me indicating that his young daughter was talking with "her friend" which would follow her to school, sleep with her and constantly be with her. The "friend" told her to hate her parents and her teachers and not to obey them. My wife, Sheri, fasted for three days regarding this matter. Before I left to check into the situation I told her that I'll talk to the young girl. She said don't talk to her but to her father, for that's where the problem lies. As I questioned him, I asked if he had a quiji board in the home. He indicated that he did and every night after the family went to bed he would play with it. I also took that board home to destroy. The girl no longer has her "friend" and the house is peaceful.

Soul Ties

We can be attacked by "soul ties" or the result of illicit sexual behavior. In 1 Corinthians 6:16-17 we read, "Do you not know that he who unites himself with a prostitute is one with her in body? For it is said, the two will become one flesh." This "one flesh" is also known as soul ties which must be broken before one can have peace. I have ministered to persons in this situation; their burden is great.

The only way to relieve their minds is to ask forgiveness for sinful deeds – and then *repent*. A person can ask many times for forgiveness regarding the same deed but that does not help. It must be repentance, or change of heart that the Lord will honor. There are good soul ties also. These are with your spouse in marriage and are the ones the Lord honors. The negative or sinful soul ties are the kind the Lord frowns upon.

Soul Travel (Astral Projection)

I have found that it is not uncommon for some Christians, especially youth to become involved in soul travel. This is an activity where Satan really can attack (and even kill) people. The setup here is where a person chants certain words that will take him or her to their alpha level of consciousness. From there they pick up their spirit guide (demonic) and travel with their soul and spirit to any place in the world, including bedrooms.

A few years ago my team was doing an eight week seminar on spiritual warfare and deliverance. One young lady said she once was involved in this activity but then in her own words "a drastic thing happened for the demons tried to drag me into hell." Another lady told me that a man said to her that he would appear in her bedroom that night. She said, "No way, for I keep my doors locked." He said "that doesn't matter, I'll be there." And right he was, for around midnight she saw him at the foot of her bed. She had attended our spiritual warfare classes and knew what to do. She yelled out "I'll cut your cord." With those words he disappeared. What cord? An unseen (with natural eyes) silver cord attaches the "travelers" to their souls and spirits and when it is cut they die. Is this scriptural? Read Ecclesiastes 12, verses 6-7 to find out.

A sixty-year old man told me he can project himself over the pyramids in Egypt and view everything that is taking place there at that time. He said that he can project himself anywhere he wishes to go. A young girl who I knew that was into astral projection died and no one could find a valid reason. Was she projecting herself at that time and was prevented in returning to her body by the demons?

Only God knows. Talking to people (even Christians) who are involved in this demonic venture leads me to believe that they are putting their lives in jeopardy as they open themselves up to Satan and give him permission to operate in his "playground."

Incubus and Succubus

According to *Webster's New World College Dictionary* (fourth edition), the definition of <u>incubus</u> is "An evil spirit or demon thought in medieval times to descend upon and have sexual intercourse with women." <u>Succubus</u>: "A female spirit or demon taught in medieval times to descend upon and have sexual intercourse with sleeping men." I hate to inform the dictionary staff and consultants that although these phenomena may have occurred in medieval times they certainly are alive and prevalent to this very day.

During a television program, a lady said that the best sex she ever had was with the 'ghost' that lives in her house. Recently, I spoke at a church where the minister said to me, "Be sure you bring up incubus and succubus for I know members of my congregation are engaged in it." Joe and I were called to a Christian lady's home by her two daughters. They told us that their mom was having sex with a spirit. As we entered the house, both of the daughters jumped us. A demon from one of them called out that he was the master of the universe. Joe yelled back, "Master of the universe, I command you to come out in the name of Jesus Christ." After that all was quiet and under control. Their mother who was in her 60's said that her husband had died a few years ago and that the Holy Spirit was having sex with her now to take his place. Oh, how far are we from glory? She was quickly delivered and at last communication all three were involved in a church.

Curses And Word Curses

So often curses are done inadvertently. A parent might tell a child, "Won't you ever learn that, how stupid can you be." This plays directly into Satan's hands, for he says to the child, "See, you cannot learn, you are stupid. Even your parents tell you that." So parents, put the best construction on everything and speak positive words to your children. Speak blessings on them, not curses.

What does the *Bible* say about curses? We read in Proverbs 18:21, "Death and life are in the power of the tongue: and they that love it shall eat the fruit thereof." Deuteronomy 30:19-20 says "This day I call heaven and earth as witnesses against you that I have set before you life and death, blessings and curses. Now choose life, so that you and your children may live." Parents take heed!!

"Bloody Mary"

I have found when talking with teens that some of them play a game called "Bloody Mary." One day when I was teaching on this subject, two Christian boys indicated to me that they play this game quite often. I was called to an elementary school by the principal who told me there were some children that had "weird" problems. Upon arriving at the school I was introduced to three girls in grades three and four and their mothers. One girl had three large scratches across her face. My first response to her was, "I bet you didn't get the light on in time." She agreed. Her mother asked what was I talking about? I told the girl to explain to her mom what had happened. She said that when her friends get together, one stands in front of a mirror and another at the light switch. She then calls "Bloody Mary" and a demon comes out of the mirror, but this time the other girl missed the light switch and the demon got to her – thus the three large scratches. Another girl said she and her friends go into their basement and "call up" their grandmothers. The third girl said they levitate their friends. The girls even stated that they float chalk and chalkboard erasers around the classroom when the teacher steps out of the room. Of course all three mothers were appalled. "My daughter is doing this?" was the common response. I told them they better know what their children are doing and take some time with them before they become caught up in other demonic activities.

Porno Movies

Another avenue in which Satan works is demonstrated by a university girl who came into my office and said that all she can think about is sex. I asked what had happened. She stated that a few days ago she went to a porno movie and since then could not think of anything else. Here again, when one opens his or her mind to Satan, he will move right in.

Attacked With A butcher knife

A group of Christian ladies were meeting in a home and since I was an advisor to the group, I also was in attendance. When I went into the kitchen to help the host she attacked me with a large butcher knife. Since I was on my high school wrestling team I easily took her down to the floor and removed the knife from her hand. I asked what had come over her? She stated that she had an operation and since then wanted to kill someone with a knife. When she was under anesthetic her mind was in "neutral." Before you go for an operation make sure you pray that the Lord will protect your mind so Satan doesn't get a foothold there.

Giving Satan The "Legal Right"

When we consult astrology, horoscopes, palm reading or fortune tellers to determine our future we are breaking the First Commandment: "You shall have no other gods." Let God determine your future, not Satan. Look what the Lord says to us in Jeremiah 29:11-13 of the NIV: "For I know the plans I have for you," declares the Lord, "plans to prosper you and not to harm you, plans to give you hope and a future. Then you will call upon me and come and pray to me, and I will listen to you. You will seek me and find me when you seek me with all your heart." You give Satan the "legal right" when you consult channelers, mediums or psychics, for now he has gained another foot-hold to influence our lives.

Satanic healing is another way in which we let this deceiver get into our lives. I know of a man who broke his leg. A few days later he was already playing football.

When asked how he could get back on the playing field so quickly he said "Satan healed me." Satan may have healed him but in the process he sold his soul to the evil one. Today he has man's glory but tomorrow he'll be Satan's glory. Satan can duplicate some of God's gifts so we must have discernment as to the source. Robert Frost in his poem *The Road Not Taken* concludes by saying "…two roads diverged in a wood, and I – I took the one less traveled by, and that had made all the difference." Do we follow Satan's road or God's? The choice is yours – and it will make "all the difference."

Tarot Card Reading

Another avenue in which we open ourselves to Satan's devices is through card reading. One young man indicated to me that he was having many difficulties with his life. I discovered he was reading tarot cards and giving "audience." After I destroyed the pack his life changed for the better. Also, is table-tilting God's way of communicating to us? No way! But on one occasion I attended a Christian group meeting and this activity was underway – and of course I went my way and left this group of "Christians."

Séances, Etc.

Beware of séances and "communicating" with the dead. Ecclesiastes 9:5-6 sums this up very well by stating, "For the living know that they will die, but *the dead know nothing*; they have no further reward, and even the memory of them is forgotten. Their love, their hate and their jealousy have long since vanished; never again will they have a part in anything that happens under the sun." God does not want border-line Christians. Rev 3:16 says, "So then because thou art lukewarm, and neither cold nor hot, I will spue (vomit) thee out of my mouth." All of the above practices go against God's teachings; therefore, we must be cognizant of the wiles of the devil. We must practice spiritual warfare.

Chapter Three

What We Must Do To Defeat Satan

What To Do

Jesus is coming for a pure people – not a borderline, wishy-washy, one day good, one day bad, Sunday only type, double minded, pew-warming Christian. Here are some suggestions that we can do to prepare ourselves:

(1) pray - when we work, we work, but when we pray God works

(2) fast - my research sources list thirty-five fasts in the *Bible*. Presently there are twenty-eight listed on the Jewish calendar. Is God trying to tell us something? Read Isaiah 58

(3) get into the Word - and study it

(4) confess your sins and repent

(5) make Jesus lord over everything and central in your life

(6) praise God - He inhabits the praises of His people

(7) put on the full armor of God

(8) have no fellowship with darkness

(9) live by God's Word

(10) submit to God

(11) forgive and forget

(12) engage in right fellowship

(13) break off all negative soul ties

(14) break off any negative law of generations

(15) do not delve into the occult

(16) know Satan's devices

(17) bind Satan when he comes after you

(18) listen to what God is telling you

All of Satan's devices cannot hurt us unless we let him get to us. Close your door so he cannot get his foot in it.

Fight The Good Fight Of Faith

If we stay clean and fight the good fight of faith, pray, read the *Bible* and seek God, Satan is defeated in our lives. Check out everything with the *Bible* e.g., sermons, televangelists, printed material, etc. An example of this is found in Acts 17:11 where the noble Bereans "received the word with all readiness of mind and searched the Scriptures daily to see whether these things were so."

Which Direction Will Your Ship Go

The following poem by Ella Wheeler Wilcox in her book *Winds of Faith* provides some needed direction for us:

> *One ship drives east and another drives west*
> *With the selfsame winds that blow.*
> *'Tis the set of the sails*
> *And not the gales*
> *Which tells us the way to go.*
> *Like the winds of the sea are the ways of fate,*
> *As we voyage along through life:*
> *'Tis the set of the soul*

> *That decides its goal,*
> *And not the calm or the strife.*

How are your sails set? Which wind will they catch? What direction will you go? Again, life is made up of choices. It's your choice.

Know Your Authority

Let's look at your authority according to what the *Bible* says. In James 4:7 we read, "Submit yourselves therefore to God. Resist the devil, and he will flee from *you*." Notice the sequence here. Practice it. 1 John 4:4, "Ye are of God, little children, and have overcome them: because greater is he that is in you, than he that is in the world." Overcome whom? The agents of anti-Christ. Mark 16:17-18: "And these signs shall follow them that believe; in my name shall they cast out devils; they shall speak with new tongues. They shall take up serpents; and if they drink any deadly thing, it shall not hurt them; they shall lay hands on the sick, and they shall recover."

Jude 9 says, "But even the archangel Michael, when he was disputing with the devil about the body of Moses, did not dare to bring a slanderous accusation against him, but said, 'The Lord rebuke you!'" What powerful words for us to use! Jesus, the most powerful word in the Bible and when we combine it with our testimony we will be able to defeat everything that Satan tries to throw against us. The *Amplified Bible* brings this out by saying in Habakkuk 3:19, "The Lord is my strength, my personal bravery and my invincible army." He will support and protect us against the wiles of Satan. Thank you Jesus!

You have the authority. Are you using it? If not, why not? Also, you must have faith. There is a world of difference between faith without measure and a measure of faith. Don't have a "but" faith, have faith as the women in Mark 5:34 who had the issue of blood. Jesus said to her, "Daughter, your faith has healed you. Go in peace and be freed from your suffering."

Some Caveats From James 3:13-16

"Who is wise and understanding among you? Let him show it by his good life, by deeds done in the humility that comes from wisdom. But if you harbor bitter envy and selfish ambition in your hearts, do not boast about it or deny the truth. Such 'wisdom' does not come down from heaven but is earthly, unspiritual, *of the devil*. For where you have envy and selfish ambition, there you find disorder and every evil practice." Here's where you come under the influence of Satan.

Remember that Jesus has a plan for your life – but so does Satan. If you have rats in your garage, how will you get rid of them? Poison some, trap some and maybe shoot a few, but what happens again? Yes, the rats will return. The answer is that you must clean the garbage out so they will not return. The same holds true for our lives. Clean the garbage out and the demons will stay away.

The Crux Of Spiritual Warfare

In the Gospel of Matthew 16:22-23, Jesus tells His disciples that He's going to die, but "Peter took him aside and began to rebuke him. 'Never, Lord!' he said. "This shall never happen to you!" Jesus turned and said to Peter, "Get behind me, Satan!" Interestingly, Jesus did not tell Peter to "get behind me" but he said those words to Satan who was influencing him to challenge Jesus. This leads us to the following three pivotal verses of spiritual warfare.

Binding Satan

(1)We read in Matthew 12:29, "How can one enter into a strong man's house, and spoil his goods, except he first *bind* the strong man? and then he will spoil his house." (2)Then Mark 3:27 says, "*No man* can enter into a strong man's house, and spoil his goods, except he will first *bind* the strong man; and then he will spoil his house." (3)Finally in Matthew 16:19 Jesus says, "And I will l give unto thee the keys of the kingdom of heaven: and whatsoever thou shalt *bind* on earth shall be bound in heaven: and whatsoever thou shalt loose on earth shall be loosed in heaven." Bind, bind, bind. Those are powerful words to use when you come against Satan in the name of Jesus.

Since we have God's authority over Satan we can say, "Satan I *bind* you in the name of Jesus. You cannot come against me, my family, my finances, etc…" Try it, it works. God gave this power to us but I am sad to say that many Christians do not even try it – or know that they *can* use it, or even think they have the power to bind Satan.

Luke 10:19 also gives us authority by saying, "Behold, I give unto you power to tread on serpents and scorpions, and over all the power of the enemy: and nothing shall by any means hurt you."

CHAPTER FOUR

Examples Of Binding Satan

Walter

Walter, a college student, called me two weeks before his Christmas break and said he was not excited about going home since his mother was an alcoholic. I told him he didn't have to put up with that. He asked what could he do? My response to him was that every day he should say "spirit of alcohol and Satan, I bind you that you cannot use your power against my mother, in the name of Jesus. Lord Jesus convict my mother and turn her to you." After his vacation, Walter returned to college. At 6:00A.M. that same morning he called and said when he went home his mother told him that something funny was happening for the whisky all tasted like vinegar and all that remained in the house to drink was ginger ale. He also mentioned that his dad told him that this is the first time in fifteen years that he had a wife. I asked Walter what did he do? His reply was "I did exactly what you said and bound Satan every day over my mother. It worked."

School Teacher's Testimony

A classroom teacher for eighteen years said that this was the worst class she ever had in her life. I told her I could solve that problem if she would go into her classroom and bind Satan every day, commanding him that he *will not* influence the children in any way; then ask God to come into the room and give them peace and tranquility. Three months later I saw her and asked how things were going? Her response: "This is the best class I have ever had." I asked what happened? She said she bound Satan every day but initially didn't believe it would work – but now she's a believer. Note: from the worst classroom to the best.

Welfare Department Worker

One Sunday I gave a presentation at a church where there was a welfare worker in attendance. Part of my presentation was on how to bind Satan. The next week I returned and she asked if she could give a testimony. In such cases you do not know what is about to happen, but she mentioned to the congregation that "what that man said really works." She went on to say that her office is a rough place to work and not much peace and joy take place there, so every morning she bound Satan when she came into her office. She then said, "This was the best week I've ever had." She bound Satan and asked the Lord to instill an attitude of peace and tranquility in her office. Her closing remark was –"It works."

Destroy The Whisky Bottles

One woman in a country church where I had just given a spiritual warfare presentation told the congregation she bound Satan for two weeks so he could not use his power against her husband and asked Jesus to convict him of his alcohol habit. One evening she heard the breaking of glass in the basement and went to see what was happening. Her husband was breaking the bottles and pouring the whisky down the drain. All he said was "I'm off of it." She didn't tell him, but she knew what the catalyst was behind the breaking of his habit.

No More Nightmares

One sixty-year old lady told me she had nightmares every night. Often times she would wake up screaming. After binding Satan she never has had one since. She bound Satan and said to God if anything enters her mind during her sleep, let it be of Him. She testified many times about the change that had taken place and how she removed Satan from her night dreams. She too, testified as Walter, the classroom teacher and the welfare department worker in the examples above that it works!

"It Is My husband"

At a Christian meeting, a couple came up to Joe for ministry. The wife said that her husband needed deliverance but the Lord told Joe it was his wife that needed it. When he prayed, the demons immediately were released from her. Joe discerned her demons by what the Holy Spirit was telling him. The moral of this story is don't tell others they need deliverance when *you* need it

"I Never Knew Him"

Another time, a woman came forward for deliverance during Joe's ministry. She was a Christian for thirty years and regularly attended church but the Lord told Joe that she was not saved. After she was set free she stated to Joe, "I never knew Him," so he prayed a prayer of salvation with her and she asked for forgiveness and for Jesus to come into her life. I've often wondered how many people are sitting in the pews that have no relationship with Jesus? Satan fools these people, for they think they are saved simply by going to church or being part of a certain denomination. Salvation is achieved with our relationship, love and commitment to Jesus. He will never leave us, but the case always is that *we* leave Him. Christianity is both a religion and a relationship.

You Have To Have "The Want To"

Joe, Bud and I ministered to a teen-aged girl who would go into cemeteries and "talk" to her dead friends. She could not even say the name of Jesus or the blood of Jesus. The demons were in full control of her for she was possessed and had to be carried into the church for ministry. She had no control over any thoughts, words or actions and was deeply involved in soul travel. She ran from church member to church member saying evil statements about the pastor, thus turning most of the congregation against him. She, along with Satan reduced the number from fifty people to less than ten.

The Lord explains what He does with such people in Romans 1:28, "And even as they did not like to retain God in their knowledge, God gave them over to a reprobate mind to do those things which are not convenient..." She was destroying herself and taking others with her. God comes to join, Satan comes to separate. We tried to minister to her but she retained the demons, so finally Joe went to the hospital psychiatric ward and delivered her by commanding the demons to say the name of Jesus. She was then set free. One point to remember when talking to the demons, if they respond verbally to you say, "Will that statement hold up before Jesus? I command you to tell me if that is true in the name of Jesus."

"I Have Lust For You"

I was speaking and ministering at a Christian meeting when a young woman came to me and said that she had lust for me and would like to spend some time together after the meeting in the hotel where the meeting was taking place. Immediately, the Lord impressed to me that she had demons that helped her find men. I told her she could be delivered but instead she wanted to keep her desire and sin, at which point she turned around and left the meeting. The Lord will not deliver you if you still have the desire to retain sin in your heart and in your life and prefer a life of bondage under Satan's control. The Lord will help if you confess and repent of your sins; then He will set you free – that is only if you want to, but I have found that sometimes the people prefer to keep their sin. The choice is yours.

The Most Bazaar Case

One of the strangest cases Joe and I have ever encountered was when a grandmother called us to her home to minister to her grandson. I sensed that this would be a difficult situation so I called the town's police department and asked if an officer could be present. The chief consented and sent an officer just in case any problems would occur. The boy's father was in the occult. As we walked into the kitchen all of a sudden the stove turned on. While we were talking to the boy and grandmother the computer printer turned on and printed a picture of a demon, after which the dog house with a small dog in it came rolling out of a bedroom into the living room where we were sitting.

Tongues of fire were all over the living room carpet and every place the boy stared a fire would break out. The carpet had burn marks in numerous places. The boy said that the computer would often turn on and print messages to him; also, a coin came rolling out of a room at us. This was poltergeist. The grandmother was also in the occult and used this encounter as a "training period," for the boy wanted to be a warlock. When they would go shopping, the cans would jump off of the shelves into their basket. As a result no ministry could take place. As we left, a dog was howling like a wolf on the front porch. The police office said that this was the most bazaar case he had ever seen.

Demonic Shadows

A man befriended me because he thought I was in the occult and that I had the powers that went along with it. He would go into cemeteries at night and photograph "spirits." Having a chest full of demonic pictures, he showed me his shots in which there were shadows floating around the tombstones. He stated that in his home his mother-in-law's chair in which she was seated would rise to the ceiling. His basement was used for devil worship which included a quiji board. There was a house nearby where a girl was murdered so he would take pictures of the demons that were peering out of the third floor windows. He sold them to a certain magazine that purchased these demonic pictures. He wanted me to go to Hollywood to help him produce a film about the actions of demons but it never came to fruition.

Joe and Bud were at a restaurant with a friend who said he had the ability to read minds and that he knew what anyone was thinking. He wanted to read Joe's mind but Joe did not take to this and bound Satan and all the demons that were involved. The man told them that it always worked in the past but for some reason that night it didn't for he drew a blank. All you have to do is use your authority that Jesus Christ gave you. It works.

Demonic Influence On Children

Where do you think the inspiration came from for this three-year old girl? Joe was telling of a child he knew who cannot write cursively, but when the demons control her with automatic writing, she can do a beautiful job of almost perfect calligraphic quality. Young children can also be influenced by demons.

One twenty-year-old lady came to me for deliverance and stated that she had demonic problems from the age of six. I asked her what had happened at that time. She stated up until then her parents were Christians and prayed for her, but eventually they got into porn, sex and other kinds of sin so they quit praying and at which time she knows that the demons entered her. She was delivered but for fourteen years she struggled with her actions and thoughts until set free. Grandparents and parents, pray for your children. They need the covering and protection of Jesus at all times.

My deliverance team has found in some cases if a child is unwanted, abused or uncared for that there are three prince demons that can influence him or her. These are the demons of rejection, rebellion and bitterness. We have encountered these three in children a number of times. Parents please take note!

What Jesus Says About Little Children

Jesus does not leave out the little ones. In Matthew 19:14 He says, "Let the little children come to me, and do not hinder them, for the kingdom of heaven belongs to such as these," and in Mark 9:37 He says, "Whoever welcomes one of these little children in my name welcomes me; and whoever welcomes me does not welcome me but the one who sent me." Also, protection comes from the angels, for in Matt 18:10 Jesus says, "See that you do not look down on one of these little ones. For I tell you that their angels in heaven always see the face of my Father in heaven." Pray, pray, pray, and teach your little ones about Jesus and how He loves them. Do it at their earliest understanding.

A Complete Turn-Around

Although there are many more examples that could be included, this one is another team-involved happening. As I was speaking at a Christian meeting a young women charged down the aisle screaming and yelling and exhibiting fingers that looked like claws. I quickly called out that I needed four men, one on each limb. Joe and Bud and two others grabbed her as she tried to bite herself and fight us. She proved to be extra strong with her demonic power and the four men struggled to hang onto her. I prayed and bound the spirits that had taken over her.. All of the demons soon were removed. In such cases it is wise to bind the person's strength and the demonic strength, commanding them that they cannot get any outside help. When they are bound their force is negated. Here is another example why it is a good idea to work in a team or as a unit, for in instances as this extra help is needed. The Lord always uses input from each member of the team in this ministry.

Joe saw this same young women a few years later when she was preaching about Jesus to a large group of people at a local park; later he saw her attending church. He went into the local Christian bookstore and saw her name printed on a poster whereby she was holding meetings and speaking at various sites throughout town. What a change from demonic filled to Spirit filled. He continued to attend some meetings and ministered with her. This proves that your work in the Lord is not in vain as demonstrated by Joe as he continued to be led by the Lord in his ministry. Always be prayed-up and fasted-up so the Lord can use you at any time or any place.

Demons Can Break Windows

One afternoon I was speaking at a restaurant to a group of Christian ladies. When I got up to speak, I called out "If there are any demons in this room I bind you and command you to leave in the name of Jesus." All of a sudden we heard one of the back windows break. The ladies jumped up thinking they would be covered with glass, but it didn't shatter for only a bowling ball size piece of glass broke outwardly in the shape of a perfectly round hole. The entire window did not break. One lady who was seated next to that window said it looked like a glass-cutter had come and cut a round hole in the window. It shocked everyone.

I asked the Lord what happened? He spoke to me loud and clear stating that this is what happens when you bind the demons and cast them out, *they will go*. What a real demonstration as to what happens when you take authority over Satan and his demons. I am sure these ladies got the true message and an education on how to bind and cast out Satan and his minions. Years later, I saw some of these same ladies and they brought up this happening again. What an impact the Lord made on the minds of these people —and also on me! I might add, after that the meeting became quite spirited. PTL!

This brings out Matthew 18:20 which says, "For where two or three are gathered together in my name, there am I in the midst of them." Another example of this Scripture occurred during the writing of this book. I taught a Confirmation class in my denomination and for the final session we had the parents of the confirmants, family, friends, relatives and members of the church gather together for a Sunday service where the youth gave their testimonies, answered biblical questions, dedicated their lives to Jesus and took Communion.

As the last confirmant kneeled down at the altar to receive Communion, the image of Jesus appeared on the wall next to them. My wife, Sheri captured this on film and made copies for each of the youth. Jesus was leaning over as in prayer which we feel was His acceptance and approval of the youth as each dedicated their lives to Him. What a way to culminate the class after a year of study!

CHAPTER FIVE

Faith And Beyond

___

The story is said of Houdini who one day was answering a dare, allowed a boxer to hit him full force in the stomach. But Houdini's timing was a split second off and the boxer's fist slammed into him before he was prepared. Houdini reeled but managed to regain his composure. "Not that way" he coughed, "I've got to get set. Now hit me." And the boxer hit again, but this time it was against an abdomen almost as hard as stone. Houdini did not even flinch.

Ten days later Houdini died from the injury inflicted by the boxer's first blow. He had not been sufficiently prepared. It's a dreadful feeling not to be ready for the temptations and problems that face us on a day-to-day basis. So the first step is to be prepared, but how do we do this? Much of our preparation is spiritual. We must get into a daily habit of studying the *Bible*. Only Jesus and His Word can defeat Satan.

How can we expect to have strength and power from God unless we are students of His Word? So this is the first step in confident living – be prepared and that comes through your devotion to your relationship with Jesus. So often we can find time to watch TV, work on projects, do trivial things and read books and magazines, but where should our real interest lie? What should we be doing? Psalm 34:8-9 says, "Taste and see that the Lord is good; blessed is the man who takes refuge in him." And in Jeremiah 33:11 we read: "Give thanks to the Lord Almighty, for the Lord is good; his love endures forever." Nahum 1:7 says, "The Lord is good, a refuge in times of trouble. He cares for those who trust in him." Give heed to these Scriptures and you will be blessed.

Our Mind: The Battleground

We hear so much about spiritual warfare and how to defeat the devil. However, we don't realize that the most dangerous battleground is our own mind. It is here that most of the battles are fought and won or lost. It is here where the enemy attacks and divides. It is here that we must continually renew our minds and bring into captivity those thoughts contrary to God's Word. Submitting requires developing an intimate relationship with God, that is learning His desires, thoughts and His will. We must seek to know the very heart of God.

The Lord loves you and desires more than anything an intimate relationship with you whereby He can reveal His love and plan for your life. Seek the heart of God so that you might be one with Him as He and the Father are one (John 10:30). Walking in love is the true way of submitting to God. We may have committed the golden rule to memory but what we really need to do is to commit it to life. Satan cannot deal with love. Jesus always walked in love. He stated that is the way the world would recognize us. Remember the anecdote to the devil's snares is love: *God's love*. It is only when we submit to, and nurture that love can we become the vessel He planned for us to be to combat the enemy. If this is difficult to do by yourself, call upon a trusted friend that you can rely on to help you in your time of need – one you have confidence in and one who will not repeat to others any problems that you might have.

Many Christians are an undisciplined regiment in the Lord's army. They do not train or discipline themselves to prepare for the battles of life; therefore, they are unprepared when the attack comes or when God calls them to the front lines. Without the discipline that is inherent in a personal relationship with the Lord we will unsuccessfully battle the enemy without the full armor God provides. We are only as strong as the weakest link in our armor. The dictionary is the only place you'll find the word "discipline" before the word "prayer."

Two Natures

Even the birds can teach us a lesson. The cowbird never builds its own nest. It finds a nest of eggs with the mother gone and lays an egg in it. The other bird cannot count so it hatches and also feeds that baby bird. The cowbird grows to be larger than the other birds and soon forces them out of the nest, killing them one at a time until it has strength to fly away on its own. Paul teaches us, spiritually speaking, that we have two natures in one nest also. The nature that we feed will grow. The nature that we starve will diminish. Which nature are you feeding?

The battles are His and He has already won the war. Rest in that provision for your life. Remember that God's peace is victorious spiritual warfare. Hold that peace, live in obedience, walk in God's love and you will win the battles and the war. Read Romans 7:21–8:16 about sin and the flesh and how we are "heirs of God and co-heirs with Christ." Then in Matthew 24:13 we read, "He that endures to the end shall be saved." To gain the victory bind Satan and pray that Jesus would come in and take care of the situation and take complete control of your body, soul, spirit, thoughts, words and deeds. Become one with Him. He will give you His all. I asked Pastor Hoard when did the Holy Spirit come upon him and give him his many gifts. Bud's response: "When I gave Jesus my all for His all." He then put his entire life and ministry into the hands of the Lord and is a dynamic member of our deliverance team. Your all for His all! What a great exchange.

It Takes Faith -We Must Have It, Hold Onto It, And Demonstrate It

Satan despises our faith that we have in Jesus, for if he can take that away from us and we begin to doubt the power we have in the name of Jesus, then the devil has a foothold in our lives. In 1Timothy 1:18-19, Timothy was told to hold on to faith and a good conscience. May we do the same. The word "faith" occurs twice in the Old Testament and 245 times in the *King James Version* of the New Testament. There are different kinds of faith:

Common faith – Titus 1:4
Little faith – Matthew 6:30
Temporary faith – Luke 8:13
Unwavering faith – James 1:6
Faith combined with works – James 2:17
Receiving faith – Romans 10:17
Great faith – 1 Timothy 1:5 and 2 Timothy 1:5
Faith and hope – Hebrews 11:1

Faith Will Move You Into:

Salvation – Ephesians 2:8-9
Answered prayer – Matthew 21:31-32 and Mark 11:23-24
Healing – James 5:14-15
Strong, unshakable walk with God – 2 Corinthians 5:7
Victory – 1 John 5:4
Holy life (preservation unto salvation) – 1 Peter 1:5

You have these two choices in life: trying to do things in your own strength and ability or doing things through faith with God's strength and His ability. The ways divide here. The choice is yours and will make all the difference. Which way will you choose? James 1:6-8 says "When he asks, he must believe and not doubt, because he who doubts is like a wave of the sea, blown and tossed by the wind. That man should not think he will receive anything from the Lord; he is a double-minded man, unstable in all he does."

An example of faith is when a pastor told his congregation that the following week they would gather to pray for rain. When the prayer-time took place, a little girl came to church with an umbrella. That's faith! It's a down payment of things desired, a guarantee of answered prayer, a shield of armor with confidence in things to come and in Hebrews 11:1, evidence of things not seen. Faith always anticipates. Do you look ahead? Do you have enough faith to anticipate? Do you see meaning in your life? Faith and trust can answer all of these.

Faith dares. Do you step out to pray for someone? Do you encourage others? If someone is not healed for whom you've prayed, do you quit praying for others? Even if you're persecuted do you continue when it is right? Overcomers shall inherit the Kingdom of God. A personal example of faith comes from Sheri and my little dog, Woofie. He comes running to us and jumps up into our arms. He trusts that we will catch him; otherwise, he will tumble to the ground. That's faith, that's trust. That's the kind of faith we should have when we come to Jesus. Faith and spiritual warfare come together especially when we minister to others in deliverance.

CHAPTER SIX

Breaking Down Strongholds And Basics Of Deliverance

W hat was Jesus' first act to start his ministry in Mark? That Gospel (1:23-27) says it was to cast out an unclean spirit *in the synagogue.* Today that terminology would mean the church. It took the disciples at least one year to know who Jesus was, but the demons knew Him immediately. Now some people live a lifetime and still don't know who He is.

We Have That Power

Do you believe? Then you have the power to overcome and be victorious. If you feel you don't then you probably don't have His power for anything else either. Let's look further in Mark 6:7, "And he called unto him the twelve, and began to send them forth by two and two; and gave them power over unclean spirits."

Luke 13:11 (KJV) mentions a certain women who came to Jesus. "And, behold, there was a woman which had a spirit of infirmity eighteen years, and was bowed together, and could in no wise lift up herself." In verse 16 Jesus continues by saying, "And ought not this woman, being a daughter of Abraham, *whom Satan hath bound,* lo, these eighteen years, be loosed from this bond on the Sabbath day?" A follower of God, bound by Satan, but set free by Jesus. That too, is the power we have in His name.

Another example is when "the seventy returned again with joy, saying, Lord, even the devils are subject unto us through thy name" (Luke 10:17). This power now has been given to us. Use it!

Even Many Ministers Do Not Believe There Are Demons

In one church where I had spoken, I was told that a man came crawling down the aisle hissing and wreathing like a snake. Someone called out that this man needs deliverance but the minister's response was "He is only expressing his personally." The congregation knew more about demons than he did. In another church, the minister told his congregation that "Dr. Reck will never speak here again because he believes that Christians can have demons." Where was I at that very moment? – casting out demons in one of his church members in the name of Jesus *in front of his eyes*! Oh, how often the "elect" can be deceived.

In another church, the minister told his board that I will never speak there again for the same reason. Well, after that minister left the church the board asked me to speak – and I had twelve Wednesday night sessions with the congregation on spiritual warfare, deliverance, satanism and the occult. As I was preparing this book, another pastor told me not to talk about demons because "deliverance was for a difference society, but not for ours today."

I cannot rationalize that so-called "informed clergy" do not believe demons can harass and oppress Christians. In all of my thirty- five years (and almost one-hundred combined years among the four members of my team) most of the people the Lord has delivered through us have been "demonized." By this I mean there are areas that they cannot control. Maybe they are bombarded by thoughts of lust, hatred, violence, etc., but have control over most other areas of their lives. If they cannot control their thought-life they need to look into the problem. We do not minister to non-Christians in deliverance but only with Christians that have a desire to be set free and are willing to give all things over to Jesus, for only in His name can they be set free. I guess some ministers forget to read 1 Timothy 4:1 which says, "Now the Spirit speaks expressly, that in the latter times some shall depart from the faith, giving heed to *seducing spirits, and doctrines of devils.*"

Have we defeated Satan? If you believe so, please re-read Chapters One and Two again. Satan cannot defeat us but he sure can help us defeat ourselves and vice versa. Remember, God has a plan for us but so does Satan and in many cases Satan is the victor.

Why Some People Do Not Get Delivered

(1) unforgiveness of self and others

(2) lack of repentance

(3) failure to break off sin

(4) not ready - Jesus gave us power over Satan but our will sometimes gets in the way

(5) center of attention - desire attention

(6) failure to confess sin

(7) look at Moses in the conflict between Israel and the Amalekites; arms up equaled victory; arms tired and down brought defeat (Aaron & Hur held them up). The same principle can happen to us when we get tired and let our guard down. We must keep our guard up constantly.

(8) don't know spiritual warfare

(9) have curses on them – brought on by forefathers, self, parents or others

(10) have no desire to pray, fast or get into the Word

(11) dabble in things not of God

(12) involvement with ungodly people

(13) desire to retain sinful traditions

(14) others, as delineated in Romans 1:21-32

Many of our problems are a result of our own doing, e.g., decisions and choices (examples: no coat and catch cold, unwise purchasing then blame it on Satan).

Many times we use Satan as an excuse when really the problem stems from our own lack of, or poor judgment. The Lord gave us a mind but we are free moral agents to decide how to use it. Sometimes we make hasty decisions without much thought (as impulsive buying), then when they don't work out we pass the buck and use Satan as a scape goat. Remember, you have control over Satan so our lack of judgment generally is because of us. Sometimes people need professional counseling to help them cope with everyday life and to work out their problems. I have referred people to them when it is not a deliverance issue. Also, some health problems may stem from medical issues as chemical imbalances, thyroid problems or other physical malfunctions, so all aspects affecting life and behavior must be considered.

Strongholds In Our Lives

No aspect of spiritual warfare is more important than the tearing down of strongholds. Again, it's whom we let control our thoughts and actions. As long as strong-holds remain entrenched in us we will continue to be defeated. By strong-holds Paul is referring to our thoughts and mind, for these are associated with how we feel, think and behave. He uses the word "stronghold" as spiritual fortresses in our lives where Satan can live and where we allow him to be protected. These fortresses exist not only in individuals but also in churches, communities, governments and nations. Even though we have salvation we can still hang onto them.

Paul says to us in 2 Corinthians 10:3-4, "For though we live in the world, we do not wage war as the world does. The weapons we fight with are not the weapons of the world. On the contrary, they have divine power to demolish strongholds;" and in 2 Peter 1:3-4, "His divine power has given us everything we need for life and godliness through our knowledge of him who called us by his own glory and goodness. Through these he has given us his very great and precious promises, so that through them you may participate in the divine nature and escape the corruption in the world caused by evil desires."

Crucify Our Flesh

We must crucify our flesh daily. Jesus is not in flesh for Paul says flesh is at enmity against God; therefore, other strongholds may be gambling, pride, pornography, exploitation (taking advantage of people because of their weaknesses), etc. If you use deceit, intimidation, manipulation, hostility or rebellion to get your way you may be controlled by these strongholds. Satan can take these and make slaves of us by breaking down our lives, destroying our security and pulling us away from God and shattering our peace. They must be confronted. So often we do not realize that what is happening since they can come upon us before we understand what is taking place.

Wherever there is willful disobedience to the Word of God there is spiritual darkness and the potential for demonic activity. Give Satan legal access and he can traffic in any area of darkness, even the darkness that still remains in some Christian hearts. When we fail to destroy strongholds we allow some measure of demonic influence to infiltrate our minds as jealousy and selfish ambition. There you find bondage to Satan and he has your mind in his grips.

Don't depend on human intellect to defeat a stronghold. Proverbs 23:7 says, "As a man thinks in his heart, so is he." Jesus broke the strongholds, for Colossians 2:15 says, "And having disarmed the powers and authorities, he made a public spectacle of them, triumphing over them by the cross." He has given us examples on how to handle Satan by breaking into his house to free us. To reiterate this important verse: "For this purpose the Son of God was manifested that he might destroy the works of the devil." (1 John 3:8).

Jesus stood fast, resisted and overcame. Now we can use His power to stand fast, resist, overcome, conquer and bind Satan whenever he comes against us. Each time we defeat him the stronger we become and the stronger our faith becomes. Faith is a fruit of the Holy Spirit. Fruit doesn't ripen overnight and neither is our faith consummated in one night, so hang in there and "fight the good fight of faith." To be forewarned is to be forearmed and that is what this book is about.

How To Overcome Strongholds

(1) You have to have the "want-to." Both in spiritual warfare and deliverance the attitude of your mind is the major difference. In a number of cases, deliverance could not take place either because the person was not prepared or did not have the desire to change. This is the first step in any ministry. You cannot be "forced" to overcome if you still have the desire to continue in your old ways.

(2) Identify and analyze your attitude or problem - what can you do and what do you need the Lord to do? Ask yourself why do you feel this way? What is causing this emotion? Maybe something as simple as getting more rest or sleep or eliminating stress could solve it. Illnesses can be caused by your mental state, attitudes, stress, or tension. Attitudes affect physical, mental and emotional health. Analyze your mental state. Do what you can do and the Lord will do the rest.

(3) If you have done this and the problem still exists then take your problem to the Lord - and *leave* it there with Him. Trust for a little and you get a little. This is difficult for many Christians for they want to take the problem back immediately and not give the Lord time to work on it.

(4) Have godly habits and don't let Satan and his demons get a foothold in your life. Reject and bind temptation.

(5) Try fasting. Read Isaiah 58:8-11.

(6) If you have fear, the New Testament says numerous times do not fear. Read Psalm 23, 27, 34, 37, 91 and believe them. Jesus says I will never leave you or forsake you. When fear sets in you are actually doubting His word. Faith is believing it, living it and practicing it.

(7) Don't be intimidated. Satan tells you that you are less than other people or that you're defeated, so your self-concept is destroyed or you feel that you can't be forgiven. He works to destroy your mind. If you believe those lies you *are* defeated, for you are a priest and a king. Jesus has defeated Satan for you and now you can use His power to run Satan out of your life. Get tough

with him; you can't be a pansy. Rise above your depression, for you are a child of Jesus. Be happy and take control of yourself, practicing what Jesus said in the *Amplified Bible* version of Matthew 11:28-30, "Come to Me, all you who labor and are heavy-laden and overburdened, and I will cause you to rest. [I will ease and relieve and refresh your souls.] Take My yoke upon you and learn of Me, for I am gentle (meek) and humble (lowly) in heart, and you will find rest (relief and ease and refreshment and recreation and blessed quiet) for your souls. For My yoke is wholesome (useful, good - not harsh, hard, sharp, or pressing, but comfortable, gracious, and pleasant), and My burden is light and easy to be borne."

Seven Weapons To Use Against Satan

(1) The blood of Jesus. I asked one demon what he despised about the blood of Jesus. It stated "It's so warm, so red, it covers everything and I can't get through it." The following Sunday at a local church, a message was given by a man who said, "Make sure you cover yourself with the blood of Jesus, because it's so warm, so red, it covers everything and the demons cannot get through it." The exact order that was told to me. Now that's verification.

(2) The name of Jesus. There's no more powerful word or name upon this earth than "Jesus." Even the demons tremble when His name is spoken. In deliverance, if you try to call out demons without using His name what will happen? Nothing! They will only come out when His name is used. There is no other way.

(3) The Word. The *Bible* has sold more copies than any other book in history but how often is it opened in many Christian homes? There is an old country and western song with lyrics of "dust on the *Bible*, dust on the Holy Word." In Russia, the people would flock to get a *Bible* and they actually helped distribute them. During my three visits, there was only one man who did not accept a *Bible* from me. Never did I see any in the dumpsters or disposed on the sidewalks. On one dark and snowy night an

elderly woman came to us pulling a sled. She said there was not even one *Bible* in her village so we piled as many boxes of *Bibles* that would fit on her sled and off she went, alone on a seven mile journey back to her village on that dark and snowy December night. There was no road, only a trail that she had to follow. I commend this woman and the people of her village for their desire to read the Word.

(4) Prayer. This is the ultimate communication with God. Since the prayer time we spend with God is so brief, no wonder so many Christians say that God does not talk to them. This is why we were created; to fellowship and communicate with Him. How does your prayer time stack up? Do you think that He is satisfied with the time you spend with Him? Is your communication more than just asking petitions?

(5) Praise. Since God desires the praises of His people, one should not omit this from his or her daily prayer life. 2 Samuel 22:50 brings this out by saying, "Therefore I will praise you, O Lord, among the nations; I will sing praises to your name." We also find in 1 Peter 2:9-10, "But you are a chosen people, a royal priesthood, a holy nation, a people belonging to God, that you may declare the praises of him who called you out of darkness into his wonderful light."

(6) Witness. This is a way to show God's love to others. If a person rejects your efforts, don't be discouraged, it's God he or she is rejecting.

(7) Our testimony. Let others know what Jesus means to you. Remember, the Great Commission is not a suggestion but a command. *You* go out! Jesus reminds us in Matthew 28:18-20 when He says, "All authority in heaven and on earth has been given to me. Therefore go and make disciples of all nations, baptizing them in the name of the Father and of the Son and of the Holy Spirit, and teaching them to obey everything I have commanded you. And surely I am with you always, to the very end of the age."

Some of the above weapons are covered in more detail in other chapters. These seven points are a reminder to do what the Word requires of us. Jesus has given you His power and authority. Use it! What better assurance can we have? Believe the promises that Jesus has set before you. Your plate is full, eat heartily, be happy, be joyful and show it, for Nehemiah 8:10 promises "Do not grieve, for the joy of the Lord is your strength." Bask in that knowledge!

Ephesians 2:1-10

"As for you, you were dead in your transgressions and sins, which you used to live when you followed the ways of this world and of the ruler of the kingdom of the air, the spirit who is now at work in those who are disobedient. All of us also lived among them at one time, gratifying the cravings of our sinful nature and following its desires and thoughts. Like the rest, we were by nature objects of wrath. But because of his great love for us, God, who is rich in mercy, made us alive with Christ even when we were dead in transgressions — it is by grace you have been saved. And God raised us up with Christ and seated us with him in the heavenly realms in Christ Jesus, in order that in the coming ages he might show the incomparable riches of his grace, expressed in his kindness to us in Christ Jesus. For it is by grace you have been saved, through faith — and this not from yourselves, it is the gift of God— not by works, so that no one can boast. For we are God's workmanship, created in Christ Jesus to do good works, which God prepared in advance for us to do." What are the good works that you're doing?

Deliverance Required In The Early Church

In the early stages of the church, deliverance was required before anyone could become a member. On page 119 of *A Lion Handbook: The History of Christianity*, Dr. Tim Dowley (the organizing editor) states: "About AD 250 the church at Rome still had only one bishop, together with forty-six presbyters, seven deacons and seven sub-deacons as well and forty-two 'acolytes' or attendants and fifty-two exorcists, readers and door keepers." Page 117 brings out the following: "More intensive preparations, including fasting, *exorcism* and blessing, immediately preceded baptism." It is sad that this policy is not followed today, for deliverance in many churches is a rite long gone and never discussed. I believe more problems in churches today would be resolved if this was accomplished. In the New Testament when people went out to evangelize they also were given power and authority over demons.

"Spiritual Warfare In The Early Church" By Dr. Paul Thigpen

Dr. Thigpen is the contributing editor to *Discipleship Journal* and a staff writer for *Prison Fellowship Ministries.* To paraphrase his informative article regarding exorcism in the early church he states that casting out demons is only one aspect of spiritual warfare, but already in the first two centuries there have been examples of exorcism. Justin Martyr (100-165) wrote that "countless demoniacs" were exorcised by Christians. Tertullian (160-230) noted that pagans allowed believers to "exorcise demoniacs" and the brilliant theologian, Origin (185-254) also affirmed that "the name of Jesus drove out myriad demons from people of his day."

Dr. Thigpen continues his article by saying that during the fourth century other Christian writers spoke of exorcism as a continuing ministry. "Making the sign of the cross was actually one of the most common ways that early Christians found to drive evil powers away. One Christian leader comments, "Demons are cowards, and they are utterly terrified by the sign of the Lord's cross, because it is the Savior, stripping their arms, making an example of them." In fact, the early church had a special office to deal with exorcism and trained exorcists were available at the local churches and all levels of the church hierarchy. "Society was so saturated with demonic influence through pagan worship and immorality that those who wished to receive baptism and join the church were expected to undergo a number of exorcisms to cleanse them spiritually. A special anointing was also given just before baptism to exorcise the devil's influences from the new converts."

The ancients viewed uninhabited places as the habitation of demons; thus, the early monks built their places of refuge in wildernesses. Their belief was why Jesus went into the desert for forty days to do battle with Satan – he was "invading the devil's turf." The ancients set up their monasteries in the desert for the same reason. They too, were invading the devil's stronghold.

Anthony (251-356) said that Christians could defeat Satan by getting into the Word, prayer, praise, fasting and almsgiving. All Christians need to have discernment because Satan can disguise himself as an angel of light. He went on to say that we need a godly humility so we can defeat Satan when we are called to do battle against him. I appreciate the research that Dr. Thigpen did in his excellent article on the history of exorcism.

Why then do so many churches today not even recognize that there are such things as demons? Why do we not want to deal with them? If not, they will deal with us. It appears that the ancients knew how to confront them more so than we by following the example of Jesus. Are we following His example today? You be the judge.

Once you know how Satan uses strongholds against us, many barriers to deliverance will be removed. Go now and do the Lord's will. Be strong in His victory!

CHAPTER SEVEN

Where Did Demons Come From

Could The Fallen Angels Be Demons – My Belief

The *Bible* does not explicitly mention the origin of demons but many theologians believe they are the fallen angels described in the Book of Revelation. Certain Scriptures may be helpful but there is no definitive proof if they are demons. I have seen some of the weirdest creatures that were demons and I wondered if fallen angels would stoop so low as to look like crows (four on a lady's back), or "stick-like" beings that look like M&M candy with "sticks" for arms and legs. I have seen them take on human form but some are so grotesque that they are appalling to look at while others are handsome and beautiful. Personally, I do not think that a fallen angel would want to enter into mankind and possibly be exorcised from a person. This I feel is "below" the activities of these angels. I believe they have "better" and "higher" things to do.

One man who was engaging regularly in sex with demons told me they are the most beautiful "people" that you will ever see. One lady on TV stated that the best sex she ever had was with the "ghost" (demon) that lives with her. The only real evidence is that God created angels and if some became the demons then only He knows. Previously, we discussed Satan being thrown out of heaven by Michael the Archangel with his angels.

Personally, I do <u>not</u> believe these two are the same, for Romans 8:37-39 says, "In all these things we are more than conquerors through him who loved us. For I am convinced that neither death nor life, neither *angels nor demons,* neither the present nor the future, nor any powers, neither height nor depth, nor anything else in all creation, will be able to separate us from the love of God that is in Christ Jesus our Lord." An interesting statement here, "neither angels *nor* demons." How do you equate this phrase?

To clarify my view, although there is nothing to say that the fallen angels cannot harass us, I believe their interest goes far beyond that. I base this on Ephesians 6:12, "For we wrestle not against flesh and blood, but against principalities, against powers, against the rulers of the darkness of this world, against spiritual wickedness in high places." (*KJV)* The *NIV* of this verse states, "For our struggle is not against flesh and blood, but against the rulers, against the authorities, against the powers of this dark world and against the spiritual forces of evil in the heavenly realms." Colossians 2:15 says, "And having spoiled principalities and powers, he made a show of them openly, triumphing over them in it."

Nelson's New Illustrated Bible Dictionary defines *principality* as a powerful ruler sometimes referring to *angels and demons.* I feel if this referred to Satan alone, the *Bible* would have used this term singularly and not plural; therefore, I equate this term to the fallen angels that are over individuals, groups of people, governments, territories, nations and directing the actions of demons. The text goes on to say, "While Christians must often wrestle against evil principalities they can be victorious because Christ defeated all wicked spirits."

Through these verses and the context in which they occur in the *Bible,* in my opinion this is sufficient evidence that demons and angels are not the same. Some may continue to debate this for years to come but I see a definite separation between the two.

The *Bible* is replete with verses dealing with Satan, fallen angels and demons – and also warning us about their behavior. Satan then, controls both the fallen angels and the demons. By delving into a detailed and intensive study of these entities and checking out each occurrence and the ramifications of each, I feel you will find my belief to be valid.

The Sons Of God

In Genesis 6:1-2,4 (*NIV*) we read, "When men began to increase in number on the earth and daughters were born to them, the sons of God saw that the daughters of men were beautiful, and they married any of them they chose." "The Nephilim were on the earth in those days — and also afterward — when the sons of God went to the daughters of men and had children by them. They were the heroes of old, men of renown." There is much debate over the sons of God as to who they really are and I'm sure this controversy will continue over eons of time.

The *Septuagint*, the Greek translation of the Hebrew Old Testament, was written by Jewish scholars in the second or third centuries before Christ. They state that the sons of God of Genesis 6 were angels. The *Book of Jubilees*, Jewish literature produced in the second or third centuries before Christ presented the same view. So did Josephus, the Jewish historian of the first century. This view was also the historic position of the early church until the fourth century A.D.

Old Testament Beliefs

The Old Testament people did not understand demons as we understand them today. They related the evil spirits as coming from God, but now we know that God allowed them but did not send them. Out of His love He sends blessing, not cursing. 1 Samuel 16:15 says, "Saul's attendants said to him, see, an evil spirit from God is tormenting you." And in 1 Kings 22:21-23 we read, "And there came forth a spirit, and stood before the Lord, and said, I will persuade him. And the Lord said unto him, Wherewith? And he said, I will go forth, and I will be a lying spirit in the mouth of all his prophets. And he said, Thou shalt persuade him, and prevail also: go forth, and do so. Now therefore, behold, the Lord hath put a lying spirit in the mouth of all these thy prophets, and the Lord hath spoken evil concerning thee." This was a lying spirit "from the Lord" as to whom Micaiah referred.

Changes In Understanding Of Demons From OT To NT

In the New Testament the doctrine of demons was better understood because Jesus often spoke about them and cast them out. His disciples and some of His followers did the same, for the seventy said that even the demons were subject to them. At times they are called "unclean spirits" as in Matthew 10:1, "And when he had called unto him his twelve disciples, he gave them power against unclean spirits, to cast them out, and to heal all manner of sickness and all manner of disease." (Also repeated in Mark 6:7).

In the *KJV* they are called "evil spirits" as in Luke 7:21, "And in that same hour he cured many of their infirmities and plagues, and of evil spirits; and unto many that were blind he gave sight." In Acts 19:12 Paul ministers to a man, "so that from his body were brought unto the sick handkerchiefs or aprons, and the diseases departed from them, and the evil spirits went out of them." I have never witnessed this type of physical healing with an anointed handkerchief, but a minister who used this method stated that he has seen it work a number of times.

Jesus' Teaching About Demons

One major ministry of Jesus was to teach about demons and the influence they can have over us; also, he gave examples of what to do with them by saying that if you believe you can cast them out. Jesus gave us the power to do this, but so often today I see Christians that are afraid to take on this gift and tackle their harassers. If Jesus had demons that tried to influence Him, then how much more we?

We have so many warnings about Satan's devices that we should be able to handle them, but so often Christians don't pay heed and think they can defeat him on their own terms. All I can say about this is "good luck." It just won't work.

You see the difference in theology, philosophy and understanding between the Old and New Testaments and how Jesus came to defeat Satan and his demons and to warn us. We have His power, but if it lies dormant and bottled up in us we certainly are going against His will in our lives. Praise the Lord, we now have the victory in our mighty Lord and Savior, Jesus Christ, King of kings and Lord of lords. If we adhere to His teaching and example we shall be free and remain free. PTL.

The word "demon" does not appear in the *KJV* of the *Bible* but the word "devil" is used fifty-five times; the word "devils," sixty times. They are referred to as evil and are bent on destroying and corrupting people mentally, physically, morally and spiritually. The *Bible* calls them unclean. They possess knowledge and physical strength well beyond that of humans and live beyond the laws of the natural realm. They are invisible but can take on many visible shapes and forms. Some can even present themselves as "humans." As previously mentioned, one women said that "her demon" could take on over one-hundred different forms.

These are Satan's henchmen and workers whose job it is to carry out his evil will. They can oppress and possess people but all are subject to be cast out in the name of Jesus – and *only* in the name of Jesus. Their final destination is Gehenna (hell) and the lake of fire where they will be thrown along with Satan and remain there for eternity, never again to harass mankind.

What Do Other Scriptures Say About Satan And His Angels

<u>Revelation 12:4</u>; "His tail swept a third of the stars out of the sky and flung them to earth."

<u>Psalm 106:36-37</u>; "They worshiped their idols, which became a snare to them. They sacrificed their sons and their daughters to demons." Pagan worship was also related to demons. Certain practices today still give homage to demons as to those mentioned in previous chapters including the worship of money, power, prestige, people, etc.

Matthew 25:41; "Then he will say to those on his left, Depart from me, you who are cursed, into the eternal fire prepared for the devil and his angels." 2 Peter 2:4-5; "For if God did not spare angels when they sinned, but sent them to hell, putting them into gloomy dungeons to be held for judgment."

Isaiah 14:12-15 (*NIV*) "How you have fallen from heaven, O morning star, son of the dawn! You have been cast down to the earth, you who once laid low the nations! You said in your heart, "I will ascend to heaven; I will raise my throne above the stars of God; I will sit enthroned on the mount of assembly, on the utmost heights of the sacred mountain. I will ascend above the tops of the clouds; I will make myself like the Most High." But you are brought down to the grave, to the depths of the pit."

Ezekiel 28:13-19 (*NIV*) also foretells Satan and his minion's future: "You were in Eden, the garden of God; every precious stone adorned you: ruby, topaz and emerald, chrysolite, onyx and jasper, sapphire, turquoise and beryl. Your settings and mountings were made of gold; on the day you were created they were prepared. You were anointed as a guardian cherub, for so I ordained you. You were on the holy mount of God; you walked among the fiery stones."

"You were blameless in your ways from the day you were created till wickedness was found in you. Through your widespread trade you were filled with violence, and you sinned. So I drove you in disgrace from the mount of God, and I expelled you, O guardian cherub, from among the fiery stones."

"Your heart became proud on account of your beauty, and you corrupted your wisdom because of your splendor. So I threw you to the earth; I made a spectacle of you before kings. By your many sins and dishonest trade you have desecrated your sanctuaries. So I made a fire come out from you, and it consumed you, and I reduced you to ashes on the ground in the sight of all who were watching. All the nations who knew you are appalled at you; you have come to a horrible end and will be no more.'" So Satan, his fallen angels and demons and their fall are predicted from Isaiah and Ezekiel to the Book of Revelation.

CHAPTER EIGHT

Demons: What The Bible Says About Them

T he following Scriptures are taken from the *King James Version* of the *Bible* with the exception of some from the *Living Bible* and the *NIV*. These are noted after the verses. In the *KJV* demons are referred to as "devils."

Satan's Fall With His Angels

<u>Isaiah 14:12-15</u> – "How art thou fallen from heaven, O Lucifer, son of the morning! how art thou cut down to the ground, which didst weaken the nations! For thou hast said in thine heart, I will ascend into heaven, I will exalt my throne above the stars of God: I will sit also upon the mount of the congregation, in the sides of the north: I will ascend above the heights of the clouds; I will be like the most High. Yet thou shalt be brought down to hell, to the sides of the pit."

<u>Ezekiel 28:13-18</u> – (verse 16) "Thou wast perfect in thy ways from the day that thou wast created, till iniquity was found in thee. By the multitude of thy merchandise they have filled the midst of thee with violence, and thou hast sinned: therefore I will cast thee as profane out of the mountain of God: and I will destroy thee, O covering cherub, from the midst of the stones of fire. Thine heart was

lifted up because of thy beauty, thou hast corrupted thy wisdom by reason of thy brightness: I will cast thee to the ground, I will lay thee before kings, that they may behold thee. Thou hast defiled thy sanctuaries by the multitude of thine iniquities, by the iniquity of thy traffick; therefore will I bring forth a fire from the midst of thee, it shall devour thee, and I will bring thee to ashes upon the earth in the sight of all them that behold thee."

Revelation 12:7-9 – "And there was war in heaven. Michael and his angels fought against the dragon, and the dragon and his angels fought back. But he was not strong enough, and they lost their place in heaven. The great dragon was hurled down — that ancient serpent called the devil, or Satan, who leads the whole world astray. He was hurled to the earth, and his angels with him."

Revelation 12:4 – "And his tail drew the third part of the stars of heaven, and did cast them to the earth."

Their Final Destination

Matthew 25:41 – "Then shall he say also unto them on the left hand, depart from me, ye cursed, into everlasting fire, prepared for the devil and his angels."

2 Peter 2:4 – "For if God spared not the angels that sinned, but cast them down to hell, and delivered them into chains of darkness, to be reserved unto judgment."

Description Of The Word "Hell"

The following information is taken from *Nelson's New Illustrated Biblical Dictionary*. Both the OT and NT, *NKJV* and the *KJV* use the word "hell" to translate "Sheol" and "Hades" for the abode of the dead. Hell as a place of punishment translates "Gehenna," the Greek form of the Hebrew word that means "the vale of Hinnnom" which was a place of child sacrifice to Baal and the fire-god Molech. Even Ahaz and Manasseh, kings of Judah were guilty of this idolatrous practice. A fire burned constantly there. Jesus used this awful scene as a symbol of hell. In His time it was a garbage dump including the dead bodies of animals and executed criminals. Dogs would fight over the garbage. In essence Jesus said if you want to know what hell is like, look at the valley of Gehenna. All who are unfit for heaven will be thrown into Gehenna (hell). This word occurs twelve times in the NT. Each time it is translated as "hell." Jesus uses the word as a place of punishment. With the exception of James 3:6 it is only used by Jesus.

In Mark 9:46 and verse 48 hell is described as a place where "their worm does not die and the fire is not quenched." Repeatedly, Jesus spoke of it as outer darkness and a furnace of fire where there will be wailing, weeping and gnashing of teeth. The Book of Revelation describes hell as "a lake of fire burning with brimstone. Into it will be thrown the beast and the false prophet ." (Revelation 19:20). At the end of the age the devil himself will be thrown into it along with death and hades and all those whose names are not written in the Book of Life. "And they will be tormented day and night forever and ever." (Revelation 20:10b). My additional comment is that there is much more said in the Bible about hell than there is said about heaven.

Demons Can Oppress And Possess People

<u>Matthew 16:22-23</u> – "Then Peter took him, and began to rebuke him, saying, be it far from thee, Lord: this shall not be unto thee. But he turned, and said unto Peter, get thee behind me, Satan…"

<u>Mark 1:23-26</u> – "And there was in their synagogue a man with an unclean spirit; and he cried out, saying, let us alone; what have we to do with thee, thou Jesus of Nazareth? Art thou come to destroy us? I know thee who thou art, the Holy One of God. And Jesus rebuked him, saying, hold thy peace, and come out of him. And when the unclean spirit had torn him, and cried with a loud voice, he came out of him."

<u>Mark 1: 34</u> – "And he healed many that were sick of divers diseases, and cast out many devils; and suffered not the devils to speak, because they knew him."

Luke 8:1-2 – (*NIV*) "The Twelve were with him, and also some women who had been cured of evil spirits and diseases: Mary (called Magdalene) from whom seven demons had come out…"

Luke 11:24-26 - (*NIV*) "When an evil spirit comes out of a man, it goes through arid places seeking rest and does not find it. Then it says, 'I will return to the house I left. When it arrives, it finds the house swept clean and put in order. Then it goes and takes seven other spirits more wicked than itself, and they go in and live there. And the final condition of that man is worse than the first."

John 13:27 - "As soon as Judas took the bread, Satan entered into him."

Acts 5:16 – "There came also a multitude out of the cities round about unto Jerusalem, bringing sick folks, and them which were vexed with unclean spirits: and they were healed every one."

Deliverance And Our Authority And Power Over Demons

Habakkuk 3:19 (*Amplified Bible*) – "The Lord God is my Strength, my personal bravery, and my invincible army; He makes my feet like hinds' feet and will make me to walk [not to stand still in terror, but to walk] and make [spiritual] progress upon my high places [of trouble, suffering, or responsibility]!"

Mark 5:8 - "For he said unto him, come out of the man, thou unclean spirit. And he asked him, what is thy name? And he answered, saying, my name is Legion: for we are many."

Mark 16:17 – "And these signs shall follow them that believe; in my name shall they cast out devils…"

Luke 9:49-50 – "And John answered and said, Master, we saw one casting out devils in thy name; and we forbad him, because he followeth not with us. And Jesus said unto him, forbid him not: for he that is not against us is for us."

Luke 10:17 – "And the seventy returned again with joy, saying, Lord, even the devils are subject unto us through thy name."

Luke 10:19-20 – "Behold, I give unto you power to tread on serpents and scorpions, and over all the power of the enemy: and nothing shall by any means hurt you. Notwithstanding in this rejoice not, that the spirits are subject unto you; but rather rejoice, because your names are written in heaven."

John 14:12 – "Verily, verily, I say unto you, he that believeth on me, the works that I do shall he do also; and greater works than these shall he do…"

Acts 8:7 – "For unclean spirits, crying with loud voice, came out of many that were possessed with them: and many taken with palsies, and that were lame, were healed."

Acts 16:18 – "…but Paul, being grieved, turned and said to the spirit, I command thee in the name of Jesus Christ to come out of her. And he came out the same hour."

James 3:19 – "Thou believest that there is one God; thou doest well: the devils also believe, and tremble."

1 John 3:8 – "He that committeth sin is of the devil; for the devil sinneth from the beginning. For this purpose the Son of God was manifested, that he might destroy the works of the devil."

1 John 4:4 – "Ye are of God, little children, and have overcome them: because greater is he that is in you, than he that is in the world."

Warnings Directed To Us

Hosea 4:6 – "My people are destroyed for lack of knowledge…"

Matthew 10:28 - "And fear not them which kill the body, but are not able to kill the soul: but rather fear him which is able to destroy both soul and body in hell."

Acts 19:13-16 – "Then certain of the vagabond Jews, exorcists, took upon them to call over them which had evil spirits the name of the Lord Jesus, saying, we adjure you by Jesus whom Paul preacheth. And there were seven sons of one Sceva, a Jew, and chief of the priests, which did so. And the evil spirit answered and said, Jesus I know, and Paul I know; but who are ye? And the man in whom the evil spirit was leaped on them, and overcame them, and prevailed against them, so that they fled out of that house naked and wounded."

2 Corinthians 2:11 – "Lest Satan should get an advantage of us: for we are not ignorant of his devices."

2 Corinthians 11:14 - "And no marvel; for Satan himself is transformed into an angel of light."

Ephesians 2:2 – "Wherein in time past ye walked according to the course of this world, according to the prince of the power of the air, the spirit that now worketh in the children of disobedience."

Ephesians 6:11-12 - "Put on the whole armour of God, that ye may be able to stand against the wiles of the devil. For we wrestle not against flesh and blood, but against principalities, against powers, against the rulers of the darkness of this world, against spiritual wickedness in high places."

1 Tim 4:1 - "Now the Spirit speaketh expressly, that in the latter times some shall depart from the faith, giving heed to seducing spirits, and doctrines of devils."

2 Tim 2:26 – (Paul speaking to Christians) – "And that they may recover themselves out of the snare of the devil, who are taken captive by him at his will."

1 Peter 5:8 – "Be sober, be vigilant; because your adversary the devil, as a roaring lion, walketh about, seeking whom he may devour."

What Must We Do

Matthew 17:15-21 - "Lord, have mercy on my son: for he is lunatick, and sore vexed: for ofttimes he falleth into the fire, and oft into the water. And I brought him to thy disciples, and they could not cure him. Then Jesus answered and said, O faithless and perverse generation, how long shall I be with you? how long shall I suffer you? bring him hither to me. And Jesus rebuked the devil; and he departed out of him: and the child was cured from that very hour. Then came the disciples to Jesus apart, and said, why could not we cast him out? And Jesus said unto them, because of your unbelief: for verily I say unto you, if ye have faith as a grain of mustard seed, ye shall say unto this mountain, remove hence to yonder place; and it shall remove; and nothing shall be impossible unto you. Howbeit this kind goeth not out but by prayer and fasting."

Acts 17:11 – "These (Bereans) were more noble than those in Thessalonica, in that they received the word with all readiness of mind, and searched the scriptures daily, whether those things were so."

Ephesians 4:27-32 - "Neither give place to the devil. Let him that stole steal no more: but rather let him labour, working with his hands the thing which is good, that he may have to give to him that needeth. Let no corrupt communication proceed out of your mouth, but that which is good to the use of edifying, that it may minister grace unto the hearers. And grieve not the Holy Spirit of God, whereby ye are sealed unto the day of redemption. Let all bitterness, and wrath, and anger, and clamour, and evil speaking, be put away from you, with all malice: and be ye kind one to another, tenderhearted, forgiving one another, even as God for Christ's sake hath forgiven you."

Romans 16:19 (Paul speaking) - " I would have you wise unto that which is good, and simple concerning evil."

1 Corinthians 12:8-10 – (Pray for the gifts of the Spirit). "For to one is given by the Spirit the word of wisdom; to another the word of knowledge by the same Spirit; to another faith by the same Spirit; to another the gifts of healing by the same Spirit; to another the working of miracles; to another prophecy; to another discerning of spirits; to another divers kinds of tongues; to another the interpretation of tongues."

James 4:7-8 - "Submit yourselves therefore to God. Resist the devil, and he will flee from you. Draw nigh to God, and he will draw nigh to you. Cleanse your hands, ye sinners; and purify your hearts, ye double minded." Notice, he will flee from you!

1 John 4:1 – "Beloved, believe not every spirit, but try the spirits whether they are of God: because many false prophets are gone out into the world."

Jude 9 – "Yet Michael the archangel, when contending with the devil he disputed about the body of Moses, durst not bring against him a railing, but said, The Lord rebuke thee." These are the same words we can use against Satan: "The Lord rebuke you."

Revelation 12:11 – "And they overcame him (Satan) by the blood of the Lamb, and by the word of their testimony; and they loved not their lives unto the death."

Results Of Overcoming

2 Chronicles 16:9 – "For the eyes of the Lord run to and fro throughout the whole earth, to show himself strong in the behalf of them whose heart is perfect toward him."

Nahum 1:7 – "The Lord is good, a strong hold in the day of trouble; and he knoweth them that trust in him."

Matt 16:19 – "And I will give unto thee the keys of the kingdom of heaven: and whatsoever thou shalt bind on earth shall be bound in heaven: and whatsoever thou shalt loose on earth shall be loosed in heaven."

Matt 24:11-13 (*The Living Bible*) - "And many false prophets will appear and lead many astray. Sin will be rampant everywhere and will cool the love of many. But those enduring to the end shall be saved."

Luke 10:18-20 (*The Living Bible*) - "Yes," he told them, "I saw Satan falling from heaven as a flash of lightning! And I have given you authority over all the power of the Enemy, and to walk among serpents and scorpions and to crush them. Nothing shall injure you! However, the important thing is not that demons obey you, but that your names are registered as citizens of heaven."

Chapter Nine

Biblical Names For Satan And Suggestions For Future Study

Who is Satan

The *King James Version* of Geneses 3:1 informs us that "the serpent was more subtil than any beast of the field which the Lord God had made." The word "subtil" (subtle) means to be deceptive, elusive, crafty, one who operates insidiously (awaiting a change to entrap), harmful by enticing, treacherous, seductive, developing so gradually as to be well established before becoming apparent. Satan means adversary or accuser.

This chapter lists twenty-seven of Satan's most common names and how these names depict his evil character. Can anything good be said about him? I have over thirty different versions of the *Bible* in my collection and I cannot find a kind word in any of them for him. His goal is to capture as many Christians *as will let him*.

Satan is mentioned in the *Bible* by a variety of names. The following list states how they depict his evil character.

For Further Study

Abaddon – Apollyon – Revelation 9:11

Accuser of brethren – Job 1:7-8 and Revelation 12:10

Adversary – 1 Peter 5:8

Angel of light – 2 Corinthians 11:14

Anointed cherub – Ezekiel 28:14

Beelzebub – Matthew 10:25 and 12:24

Belial – 2 Corinthians 6:15

Corruptor of minds – 2 Corinthians 11:3

Devil – Revelation 12:9

Dragon – Revelation 12:3

God of this world – 2 Corinthians 4:4

King – Ephesians 6:12 (ruler of darkness) and Revelation 9:11

Liar – John 8:44

Lucifer – Isaiah 14:12

Oppressor – Acts 10:38

Prince of darkness – Ephesians 6:12

Prince of devils – Matthew 12:24

Prince of the air – Ephesians 2:2

Prince of this world – John 12:31 and 16:11

Roaring lion – 1 Peter 5:8

Satan – Job 1:6

Serpent – 2 Corinthians 11:3; Genesis. 3:1, 14; Revelation 12:9 and 20:2

Enemy – Matthew 13:39

Tempter – Matthew 4:3

Thief – John 10:10

Wicked one – Matthew 13:19

Additional Further Study: Demonic Activity: Nature, Mission, Results And Manifestation

The following list describes some of Satan's devices. The Scriptures are not printed out so you can study the Word and see the context of each entry. This is your "homework" to enable you to delve deeper into the area of spiritual warfare.

Astrology – Deuteronomy 17:3

Blind and dumb – Matthew 12:22

Body sores – Job 2:7

Bondage – Romans 8:15

Cities of devils – Isaiah 19:3 and Revelation 2:13

Condemnation – 1Timothy 3:6

Confusion – 2 Corinthians 11:3 and James 3:16

Convulsions – Luke 4:35

Corruptors of the mind – 2 Corinthians 11:3

Covetousness, greed – Colossians 3:5 and 1Timothy 6:10

Deaf and dumb – Mark 9:25

Divination – Acts 16:16

Doctrines of devils – 1Timothy 4:1

Double mindedness – James 1:8

Envy – James 3:14-16

Evil spirits – Judges 9:23, Luke 7:21 and Acts 19:12

Familiar spirits – 1 Samuel 28:7; 2 Kings 21:6, 23:24; and Isaiah 8:19, 19:3

Fear – 2 Timothy 2:7

Hateful – Revelation 18:1-2

Haughty – Proverbs 16:18

Heaviness (depression) – Isaiah 61:3

Infirmity – 13:11-12

Jealousy – Numbers 5:14 and 5:30

Kill – John 10:10

Lunatic – Matthew 4:24 and 17:14-21

Lusts – John 8:44

More For You To Study: How We Get Involved

(1) Had your fortune told by the use of a crystal ball, cards, tea leaves, palm-reading, quiji board, etc., or played with these for fun.

(2) Read or followed horoscopes or any form of astrology.

(3) Been hypnotized or used hypnotism in any form.

(4) Attended a séance, spiritualist meeting or consulted a medium.

(5) Had a life or reincarnation reading.

(6) Played with so-called games of an occult nature such as Kabala, Dungeons and Dragons, etc.

(7) Sought spiritual healing other than through Jesus such as psychic healers and spiritualist mediums, charmers or magic conjuration.

(8) Involved in mind-science religions or cults.

(9) Practiced table lifting (tilting) or levitation.

(10) Practiced automatic writing.

(11) Taken mind expanding drugs as LSD, marijuana, etc.

(12) Possessed any occult or pagan religious objects as buddhas, tiki gods, religious masks, etc.

(13) Been involved in witchcraft, sorcery, casting of spells, hexes, etc.

(14) Practiced transcendental meditation or called upon foreign gods in some form of meditation.

(15) Practiced astral projection (soul travel), mind reading, telepathy, clairvoyance, thought transfer, E.S.P., etc.

(16) Read demonic references as the *Satanic Bible, Shadows of the Supernatural, Buckland's Complete Book of Witchcraft, The New Age Catalog*, etc.

These are strictly forbidden in Scripture. Occult involvement is at enmity against God and invokes His wrath, for they can affect those who practice it physically, mentally, emotionally and spiritually. Today, in many churches you don't hear much about Satan and hell, so as a result church congregations do not know how to deal with spiritual warfare. The era between the first and second coming of Jesus is a time of warfare between the kingdoms of God and Satan. Two strong powers are occupying the same territory. Even Paul made this clear that the Galatians had allowed the spirit of witch-craft to invade the church. He states in Galatians 3:1, "O foolish Galatians, who has bewitched you, that you should not obey the truth?" The Greek word here for "bewitch" means to "bring evil on a person – or mislead by an evil eye." The evil eye is a manifestation of witchcraft.

The Galatians were saved and Spirit-filled and had miracles in their congregation and yet Paul tells them they were bewitched. I sense that many Christians today are under this same control. Recognize it and deal with it before you become entrapped and fall under the control of Satan.

Evil is out there. It is all around us. A Christian minister on an airplane happened to sit next to a witch. She told him that she was fasting. He asked her what was the occasion? Her response was that she was praying to Satan to over-throw two major TV ministries (the names I will not include). To what extent will evil go to tear down those who stand up for the Lord?

Chapter Ten

Scriptures Dealing With The Occult

Although some of the following Scriptures have been used in context in preceding chapters, the following is a comprehensive listing for you to use as a quick reference regarding various occult practices. They are all in biblical book order to make them easier to locate.

Astrology

Deuteronomy 4:19, 17:3,16; 21:3,5; 33:3,5
Isaiah 47:13
Jeremiah 8:2; 19:3
Daniel 1:20; 2:2,10,27; 4:7; 5:7,11,15
Zephaniah 1:5
Acts 7:42-43

Demons (Devils) (Major Scriptures)

Matthew 4:1,24; 8:31; 12:22-29; 13:39; 15:22; 16:18; 17:18; 25:41
Mark 1:26-27; 5:1-17; 16:17
Luke 3:33-35; 4:2-13; 8:12,28-39; 9:38-42; 10:17-20; 11:14-23
John 6:70; 10:20-21; 13:2

Acts 10:38; 13:10
1 Corinthians 10:20
Ephesians 4:27; 6:11-17
1 Timothy 4:1; 3:6-7
2 Timothy 2:26
Hebrews 2:14
James 3:15; 4:7
1 Peter 5:8
1 John 3:8-10
Jude 9
Revelation 2:10; 12:3-4,9,12; 20:1-3,7-10

Divination-Obtaining Secret Or Illegitimate Information And Knowledge

Numbers 22:7; 23:23
Deuteronomy 18:10
2 Kings 17:17
Jeremiah 14:14
Ezekiel 12:24; 13:6-7: 21:1-23
Acts 16:16

False Prophets – Signs And Wonders

Matthew 12:39; 24:5,11,23-24
1 John 4:1-4
2 Thessalonians 2:9-11
Revelation 13:13; 16:14

Familiar Spirits And Mediums

Leviticus 19:31; 20:6,27
Deuteronomy 18:11

1 Samuel 28:3-9
2 Kings 21:6; 23:24
1 Chronicles 10:13
2 Chronicles 33:6
Isaiah 8:19; 19:3; 29:4

Refute Reincarnation(And Spirit Leaves Body)

Ecclesiastes 9:5-6
Luke 8:55; 23:46
James 2:26
Hebrews 9:27

Soothsayers (Fortune Tellers)

Isaiah 2:6
Daniel 2:27; 4:7; 5:7-11
Micah 5:12
Acts 16:16; 8:9

Sorcery

Exodus 7:11
Isaiah 47:9,12; 57:3
Jeremiah 29:9
Daniel 2:2
Acts 8:11; 21:8; 22:15
Revelation 18:23; 21:8; 22:15

Witchcraft

1 Samuel 15:23

2 Kings 9:22
2 Chronicles 33:6
Micah 5:12
Nahum 3:4
Galatians 5:20

Witches (Female)

Exodus 22:18
Deuteronomy 18:10

Wizards (Male)

Leviticus 19:31; 20:6,27
Deuteronomy 18:11
1 Samuel 28:3,9
2 Kings 21:6; 23,24
2 Chronicles 33:6
Isaiah 8:19; 19:3

Chapter Eleven

Your Preparation And The Deliverance Session

Preparation

Before you start the deliverance session there are a number of things you must consider. Fasting and praying are essential. It's always a good idea to fast at least one day per week to be ready for any happenings in your life, not just deliverance. If the deliverance was to be in the future, I would fast from one to three days especially if I knew the spirit of witchcraft was attacking the person. Of all the spirits I have encountered this one is the most challenging. When you fast, ask God for direction and the Holy Spirit will guide you. Advanced preparation with God's help is a necessity. There may be times when you cannot fast but still make sure you ask for the Lord's direction and He will give you "last minute instructions." If you have advanced contact with the person ask him or her also to fast and pray.

Before the session begins and depending on the circumstances, take time to meditate – don't scurry around the house doing things – take some quiet time with the Lord. Often, this is when He will reveal what He wants you to do.

Go In With Authority

The demons know if you're timid so show them "who's boss;" also, go in with forgiveness of sins. They know your sins and might even call them out to the people present at that time. I know of a few situations where this has occurred and the entire deliverance sessions were terminated. Remember, the demons are smarter and stronger than we are and know all about our activities – both good and bad. Whole ministries can be destroyed so don't give them an open door. Often times Pastor Bud calls out the demons by name and knows their function. During one speaking engagement at a Christian men's fellowship meeting as the team entered the room, Bud told a lady that it was OK for her to purchase a car. She told him she had been debating that decision for a long time. At another meeting, again as we entered the room he looked at a lady and told her that her frozen toe was healed. She was stunned, for that was the malady from which she was suffering. That's what can happen when you "sell out" to the Lord.

Don't Go In With A Set Plan

My team members and I can testify that in all of our years of deliverance we have not encountered the same situation twice. Every person is different and each has his or her own problems; therefore, you must let the Lord give you direction on how to proceed. Do not think "this is how I'll do it." If you try to deliver in your own power, you are asking for failure from the beginning. The Holy Spirit will guide you – that is if you let Him.

Bind The Demons

Bind the demons and ask for the covering of the blood of Jesus over each person present even if they are not directly involved in the deliverance. I know of instances where the demons tried to go from the demonized person into someone else in the same room. You might take hold of the situation by saying, "Satan and you demons, I bind you that you cannot use your strength against us or against (state the person's name) in the name of Jesus." Do this at the beginning of the session for it starts to loosen the hold the demons have over that person. Make sure you have a *Bible* and anointing oil readily available.

Do Not Work Alone

If possible, never work alone. Also, have a friend(s) of the person there for support and comfort. When it is feasible, have a team of people to help you with the deliverance. The Lord will work through all of them, for two or three strands are harder to break than one. Each will give assistance as to how the Lord leads them.

You have to realize that all problems are not demonic. Some people need professional help and professional counseling instead of deliverance. Use your discernment here; also, some people simply want attention and use the team for companionship. In some cases, I've referred the person to a professional counselor. I know of one lady who feigned possession and came to Pastor Hoard's church and at least three others to get recognition. She would cry "I'm set free" and actually receive contributions from those persons who felt "sorry" for her. Discernment is one of the greatest attributes one can have in deliverance; also, pray for wisdom and knowledge as to what the Lord wants you to do. The Holy Spirit will guide and direct you when you ask Him for help. Listen carefully to what He is saying to you and you will have success.

The Meeting Place

A minister's wife told me at a Christian conference that I had been to her church but she didn't come forward for prayer because in her own words, "A minister's wife should not have these problems and I did not want to come up before the congregation." At the conference, she approached my wife and me privately and asked for help. With no other people present, we took her through deliverance where she coughed and coughed as if she was going to choke; then all of a sudden a green glob or "nest" of slime came out of her mouth. She was set free, but for fear of others knowing her problems her deliverance was waylaid for months.

Be careful in selecting the meeting place. We have found the best location for a deliverance is in the person's home or a quiet place, but make sure no children, pets, outsiders or phones can interfere. Respect the feelings of the person and let him or her decide where to meet. You may ask if they would like to have a friend with them at the session. This we recommend.

I spoke at a meeting of Christian women in a home a few years ago. One lady came up for deliverance but nothing happened. I questioned her about her problems but she responded incorrectly. I wondered what had happened or if I had failed to hear from the Lord. Later, a friend of hers told me that she did have those problems but she didn't want her friends to know about them. How sad, for I know her friends would have supported her. I left the meeting but she still retained her same problems. I could have met her in a separate room but probably that would have indicated to her friends that she had problems. Honesty is the best policy but you must respect the wishes of the person. One very important aspect of deliverance is to give assurance that no information will leave the room. This gives them confidence that what occurs is private. If the deliverer would "blab" everything that takes place, the Lord would quickly close off his or her ministry.

Break The Ice

Spend some time with the person and talk of things in general before the actual deliverance. Never go into a home or a meeting and immediately confront the demons, but first put the person at ease. Be friendly and cordial as to build the person's confidence in you. Establish a pleasant atmosphere. After general discussion ask the person to tell you about his or her problems. I always say that I picture their defense as a brick wall with some of the bricks missing.

Those missing bricks are the ones we need to find, but need their help in doing so. Tell them they must be honest and expound on what problems and concerns they have that are difficult to overcome. What you are doing is finding the "legal right" that has opened the door to demonic influence. One caution: many people with demonic problems have a low self-image or concept of themselves. Don't destroy it even more. This is the time to build them up, not a time to destroy them further.

Tell them what you're going to do as led by the Lord. Ask them if they want to be set free and go through deliverance. Then lead them in a prayer of salvation including rededication to Jesus. Make sure they ask Jesus to come into their life including forgiveness of sins and repentance. If there are soul ties, generational curses or cavorting with demons as mentioned in previous chapters, pray against all of these. Remember, many problems are from "branches on the trunk." Learn to identify that trunk.

Maintain their confidence and don't condemn them. Never act shocked or surprised. Ask what Jesus means to them and have them give definite statements about who Jesus is and what he's done for them, making sure they confess their faith in Christ. The major concept of counseling that I learned in my seminary classes was to *be a good listener*. Hear them out; don't interrupt. Let them bare their heart and soul to you. But one caveat: don't let them go on and on about all their problems. This is a delaying tactic used by Satan to stall. You are in charge. Be kind but firm.

Take an occasional break. Deliverance can be tiring so don't wear everyone out. In the meantime the demons are becoming frustrated listening to the rededication of the person to Jesus and what He means to him or her. They are already starting to feel they are no longer in charge.

Take Precaution

Be cautious for sometimes before the actual deliverance persons may say they already feel free. This is a ploy by the demons to make the deliverer feel the job has already been completed. Don't count on it. It's only temporary relief, for the demons have retreated for just a short time. If there is any physical violence or problems during this period before the actual deliverance, bind it. The demons have an intense hatred of you and may use the person to be violent toward you both verbally and physically.

Joe and I were called to a church where a week before, one of the parishioners became violent, destroying the furniture in a room, beating up ten men and tossing a three-hundred pound ex-police office around like a toy doll. We went into the room the next Sunday and Joe shouted out, "I bind you Satan in the name of Jesus. You cannot use your strength against him or his strength against us!" What was the result? The man sat limp in the chair for the entire session and was soon delivered of his demons.

The ten men outside of the room who were there to carry Joe and me out were amazed that this man was completely docile and set free. This reminds me of the story in Mark 5:1-13 where Jesus cast out a legion (60) of demons from the maniac of Gadara. He too was completely set free, just as that church member. You may need to bind the demons if violence occurs. You can have the demonized person bind the demons also. This is effective for it comes directly from the person who is about to be set free.

This is the preparation period before the actual deliverance and can take a few hours so don't be in a hurry to get the job done. Many times this is the longest part of the entire session. If the preparation period is done under the direction of the Lord it can be the main part of the session for the demon's hold is becoming weaker and weaker to the point where the actual deliverance may take only a few minutes.

The Deliverance Session

Now that the stage has been set for the actual deliverance, there are two ways to approach the demons: (1) command the demons to identify themselves in the name of Jesus and you may command them to tell what they are doing to influence the behavior of the person or you could say, "Prince demon I command you to tell me the names of all the demons in this person in the name of Jesus" or (2) just command they all come out in the name of Jesus without naming themselves. This is the "easier" way and no two-way communication takes place.

You don't need to shout them out for they will come out even with a whisper. This is good especially if there are other people around as in a church setting. If the demon s curse you tell them to shut up. Let's see what Jesus told them in Mark 1:23-26, "Just then a man in their synagogue who was possessed by an evil spirit cried out, "What do you want with us, Jesus of Nazareth? Have you come to destroy us? I know who you are — the Holy One of God! 'Be quiet!' said Jesus sternly. 'Come out of him!' The evil spirit shook the man violently and came out of him with a shriek." When you tell them to be quiet in the name of Jesus, they must obey.

If the person's mind becomes befuddled, bind the spirits influencing his or her mind. Look the person directly in the eyes. By doing this the demons know that you are staring at them. Tell the person not to clench his or her teeth for the demons must use the person's mouth to talk to you if you are commanding them to do so.

Remember you are not the deliverer, Jesus is. Remember the demons are stronger and smarter than you, but with Jesus on your side they can easily be handled. Also, ask the person to command the demons to leave. This makes a greater impact on them for they hear that the person wants them gone too. I have heard ministers say that they send them to hell or to the feet of Jesus. I do not believe you can do this, for it's up to the Lord as to where they will go. Luke 11:24-26 says ""When an evil spirit comes out of a man, it goes through arid places seeking rest and does not find it. Then it says, 'I will return to the house I left.' When it arrives, it finds the house swept clean and put in order. Then it goes and takes seven other spirits more wicked than itself, and they go in and live there. And the final condition of that man is worse than the first." It is my personal opinion that when they are casted out they go looking for someone else who will open themselves up to them.

Possible Questions To Ask During Deliverance

The following questions are suggestions only and used to extract information from the person as to where his or her problems lie. You would not use all of them but be led by the Holy Spirit as to which to use. After using only a few you may already have your answer. It might be a good idea to review them before the actual deliverance just to get an idea of some possible areas in which the person may be involved.

(1) Why are you seeking ministry?

(2) Who is Jesus? What does he mean to you?

(3) Are there areas in your life that seem to be out of control? If so, what are they? How often do these occur? What seems to cause them?

(4) At times do you have an uncontrollable temper? What causes it?

(5) Do you have over-whelming images or urges of perverted sex acts?

(6) Are you presently, or have you in the past engaged in illegal sex?

(7) Were you or your parents or grandparents involved in any way with the occult such as using the quiji board, fortune tellers, astrology, horoscopes, séances, table tilting, satanism, witchcraft, divination, tarot cards, palm- reading, astral projection (soul travel) or any other form of occult involvement?

(8) Were you abused or molested as a child? About at what age? Were other members of your family also molested? By whom? Have you forgiven? If not, why not?

(9) Were you a wanted pregnancy? Was your mother married at that time?

(10) Are you taking illegal drugs, alcohol or tobacco?

(11) Do you hear voices? Inside or outside? If inside, do they become forceful? Do they seem to control you? How?

(12) Are you now, or have you ever been divorced? Have you forgiven?

(13) Do you have thoughts of suicide? Are these frequent?

(14) Have you forgiven everyone who has hurt or injured you? If not, why not? Have you forgiven yourself for things you have done in the past?

(15) Do you feel Jesus has forgiven you after you have asked Him to do so?

(16) Do you see visions? Of angels or demons? Describe them in detail.

(17) Do you feel that most people are against you no matter what you do?

(18) Are your childhood memories happy or painful? Were your parents understanding? Did they love you? Did you love them?

(19) Are you happy now? If not why not? What seems to bother you?

(20) Do you read the *Bible*? How often? Do you understand it? Do you learn from it how to live and how to treat others? How often do you pray?

(21) Do you have a friend that you can rely on that you feel you can tell anything without it being passed on?

(22) Are you willing to give up any willful sin and to renounce and give up any ties to the occult?

(23) Are you willing to turn your life over to Jesus and allow him to be Lord of your life in both your spiritual and secular walk?

(24) Are you willing to repent and ask forgiveness from Jesus?

(25) Are you willing now to confess Jesus as your Lord and Savior and invite Him into your heart and life. May we now pray for this?

Post-Deliverance Teaching

After the deliverance has taken place, teaching needs to be the next step. This follow-up is essential for the person to stay free. It must include how to remain free and what to do if Satan tries to attack again. Emphasize binding Satan over and over again, for this is one of the main ways to keep him and his evil companions at bay. Anoint them in the name of Jesus. Make sure they clean up their act and give their lives over to Jesus. This is the best way to prevent Satan from coming back again. Make sure all the rats are out of the garage (see Chapter Three for meaning). Bring out the teachings in this book and relay these concepts to the person so he or she knows Satan's tactics and how to identify and overcome them. It might be a good idea to deliver the home also at this time. Show them how to cleanse it if problems appear again. Teaching is necessary! We have power over Satan. Use it!

Groupings For Deliverance Consideration

The following is a list of groupings for consideration that may be harboring or influencing or even in a person. Usually there is more than one demon in, or oppressing that person. They seem to have a "buddy system" where a group of demons with similar "interests" work. When the "prince demon" or "doorkeeper" is allowed to enter, it brings its "buddies" in to help; therefore, when taking someone through deliverance, be on the look-out for these additional demons that may also be influencing the person.

Whatever you want to call them, be they emotions, state or frame of mind, thoughts, outlooks, beliefs, suspicions, behaviors, influences, demonic influences, moods, feelings, mental state, etc., they may (and I emphasize "*may*") be subject to demonic control. Be aware of these grouping when ministering deliverance to a person. Some of the behaviors are repeated in other categories or groupings but they are relevant to what the person may exhibit.

The following list is extracted from many sources which have attempted to group these into categories in which the deliverer needs to be aware:

Bitterness

resentment	hatred	unforgiveness	violence
temper	anger	retaliation	murder
quarreling	cruelty		

Depression

discouragement	unworthy	anxious	tense
nervous	despondent	suicide	shameful
lonely	timid	glutton	heaviness
despair	guilt	shy	greed
inadequate	hopeless	condemnation	talkative
sensitive	unfairness	frustration	defeat
dejection	hopelessness	insomnia	morbidity
frustration	incoherent	lethargy	

Domination

superiority	deceiving	control	addiction
possessiveness	legalism	bondage	lying
unclean talk	gossip	infirm	worldliness
greed	deceit	intolerance	irritability
bullying	haughtiness	arrogance	impatient
prideful	ego		

Insecurity

inferiority	condemnation	loneliness	timidity
shyness	inadequacy	ineptness	self-pity
fear of disapproval			

Paranoia

jealousy	envy	suspicion	distrust
persecution	various fears	confrontation	

Pride

ego	vanity	self-righteous	haughty
self-importance	arrogance	rationalization	

Rebellion

anger	murder	violence	selfishness
self-will	anxiousness	nervousness	compulsive
critical	suspicious	doubtful	cruel
procrastination	hostile	revenge	judgmental
distrust	confusion	unbelief	temper
stubborn	dominant	irresponsible	retaliation
hatred	resentful	spiteful	

Rejection

hatred	unreality	resentment	pouting
inferiority	bitterness	insecurity	withdrawal
fantasy	self-pity	negativism	gloom

stubborn	accusation	jealous	unteachable
fault-finding			

Sexual

prostitution	fornication	harlotry	incest
homosexuality	lust	adultery	beastality
sadism	masturbation	pornography	sensuality
masochism	fantasizing	perversion	

Strife

contention	bickering	argumentative	quarreling
fighting	hatred	back-biting	restless
determination			

Worry

Anxious	fears	apprehensive	dread
burdened	frustration	agitation	gloom
disgust	nervous	despondency	dejection
defeatism			

CHAPTER TWELVE

How To Keep Your Deliverance

A reminder: make Jesus lord over everything and have faith in Him. Seven of His healings specifically mentioning individuals in the *Bible* were on the faith of others; therefore, have your own faith but also have it when praying for others.

Paint this picture in your mind. For forty days a giant had been taunting Israel's army and shouting curses against the God of Israel. The year was 1010 B.C. The king of Israel was Saul. The giant was Goliath. According to the *Zondervan Pictorial Bible Dictionary*, Goliath was from the Philistine town of Gath but was not a Philistine himself, as he was descended from the old giant line of the Rephaim or the Anakin line. This *Dictionary* says he was eleven feet tall (all references do not agree as to his height). He had twelve toes and twelve fingers. His spear was like that of a weaver's beam.

Skeletons recovered in Palestine attest to the fact that men as Goliath once lived in that region. When Moses sent out the spies, these are the kind of people they saw. They said they are like giants and we are as grasshoppers (Numbers 13:33).

The setting for the Goliath vs David battle took place in western Judah. Israel was encamped on one hillside and the Philistines on the other with a deep, narrow valley between them. I saw this valley, but the tall hills have been worn down somewhat by erosion, so today they are more like rolling hills.

King Saul placed upon David his own armor, breastplate, sword and helmet. One version of the Scripture says, "David tried in vain to go," but Saul's armor was too heavy, so David took it off and went out to face his foe with God's armor. Here's the mighty and huge giant vs the little shepherd boy, face to face. David spoke up and said: "You come at me with sword and shield, but I come to you in the name of the Lord God of Israel. He will give me victory this day..." (1 Samuel 17:45). David took his shepherd's sling and placed a smooth stone in it. He picked up five stones (for Goliath had four brothers). Shepherds used a sling to keep wild beasts away from their flocks. Judges 20:16 says that the men of Israel could sling stones at a hair and not miss – neither did David – for he came in the name of the Lord. He had on the armor of God.

I wish that each one of us could go out and face the world wearing the armor of God as described here and by Paul in Ephesians 6. The difference in our lives would be dramatic. We would overcome temptation, discouragement, anxiety, worry, fear and many of our other problems.

Ephesians 6: 10-18

Written from Rome by Paul in 64 A.D., these verses are some of his most informative and powerful works and still so pertinent to us today in our preparation of how to defeat the wiles of Satan and his demons. Dwell carefully on each verse:

(v 10) "Finally, be strong in the Lord and in his mighty power.

(v 11) Put on the full armor of God so that you can take your stand againstthe devil's schemes.

(v 12) For our struggle is not against flesh and blood, but against the rulers, against the authorities, against the powers of this dark world and against the spiritual forces of evil in the heavenly realms.

(v 13) Therefore put on the full armor of God, so that when the day of evil comes, you may be able to stand your ground, and after you have done everything, to stand.

(v 14) Stand firm then, with the belt of truth buckled around your waist, with the breastplate of righteousness in place,

(v 15) and with your feet fitted with the readiness that comes from the gospel of peace.

(v 16) In addition to all this, take up the shield of faith.

(v 17) Take the helmet of salvation and the sword of the Spirit, which is the Word of God.

(v 18) And pray in the Spirit on all occasions with all kinds of prayers and requests. With this in mind, be alert and always keep on praying for all the saints."

What is Paul saying? Stand ready! He has taken this armament from the Roman soldiers. After they defeated an enemy they didn't take a break and relax but were ready to meet the next foe that was challenging them. They took a stand and were always prepared for another encounter. You can only do this when you are dressed in the full armor of God.

Paul goes on to say that we're not struggling against mankind but against the powers and spiritual forces that make people evil. Remember what Jesus said to Peter when he rebuked Him for saying that He was to die; not get behind me Peter, but get behind me Satan. This was the force making Peter say that to Jesus. We must continue to bind the source that is causing our problems and in the people that are coming against us under the influence of Satan.

Belt Of Truth

Paul says in verse 14 that we must put on the "belt of truth buckled around your waist." Before soldiers went to battle they tied their belts tightly around their waists. This meant that they were ready and prepared for action. To loosen the belt was to be off duty. It kept the breastplate in place and from where the scabbard was hung. (The scabbard was the sheath that held the sword). This should indicate to us Christians that we must be ready with the sword to repel the enemy.

Breastplate Of Righteousness

In Isaiah 11:5 the Messiah is depicted as wearing the belt of righteousness around His waist and faithfulness as the sash around His body. The breastplate covered the body from the neck to the thighs and was worn as a heart protector. There was also a piece to cover the soldier's back. Righteousness stands for uprightness and integrity of character.

Feet Fitted With Readiness

Readiness comes from the "gospel of peace." Flavius Josephus describes the soldier's army boots as thickly studded with sharp nails. This made it difficult to move backward. The military success of both Alexander and Julius Caesar were due in large measure to their armies having good footwear where they could travel rapidly over long distances and over rough terrain.

Closer to our time, one aspect that contributed to the German army defeat in Russia was that the Germans had summer uniforms and boots. Many men suffered frozen feet during the extreme cold in Russia during World War II. The Russians stuffed their boots with newspapers and were more able to survive the cold. The Apostle Paul knew the value of "feet fitted with readiness" which he emphasized as preparedness. The NIV says "With your feet fitted with the gospel of peace as a firm footing."

Shield Of Faith

Paul says in verse 16, "Take up the shield of faith." Barclay's translation says "Soldiers fought side by side so it was as a solid metal wall, but even a single soldier found protection behind it. After one battle a Roman soldier counted 220 darts sticking into his shield." We must extinguish the flaming arrows of the evil one. The metal shields of Roman soldiers were made of metal, while in many cases the shields of their enemies were made of woven reeds, leather or other flammable materials. The Romans lighted their arrows and watched the shields of their enemies as they burned and were useless. Then the Roman soldiers moved in against an enemy that was defenseless.

Sword Of The Spirit

After reading the above passages in Ephesians 6 did you ascertain which were the defensive and offensive weapons? All but one were defensive; only one was offensive - the Sword of the Spirit. The Sword that born-again Christians possess is the Word of God. His Word can drive off an army of demons. Just the name of Jesus alone can repel any demonic onslaught and only using His name can you drive them out.

In Hebrew, the sword actually means a scepter which refers to the mouth, so the Messiah is portrayed as one who strikes the ruthless with the rod. Elsewhere in Scripture, speech is compared to a sword. So as Jesus used words to repulse the tempter, so must we use the Word to drive away Satan. It is significant that in Matthew 4:4 Jesus quotes from Deuteronomy 8:3 referring to "every word (Rhema) that comes from the mouth of God." So what does this entire armor mean? It means that God has provided us a uniform for battle. Paul is saying with his example of the Roman army that we should not retreat, but press always onward with our armor. Take a stand, for once you retreat you've given Satan control of the battleground.

Paul concludes by saying, "And pray in the Spirit on all occasions." John 4:24 brings out the fact that "God is a Spirit: and they that worship him must worship him in spirit and in truth."

The foundation for your deliverance has been laid. Now all we must do is to build on it. In the army, soldiers do not go out on their own; they fight as a unit and need the cover of their comrades for support and backup. The church must be that cover and support. Let not the unified body of the church be lost. Praying and binding together are what we need to defeat Satan and his minions.

By developing a personal relationship with the Lord, seeking His heart and disciplining ourselves to the teaching of the Holy Spirit, we will set the stage for a victorious life. It equips us for battle, carries us to victory and provides the necessary foundation on which to build our faith.

So if you are struggling without victory, if you find loving others a chore and not a blessing and if you are in a constant state of turmoil, maybe you need to revisit basic training. Sit at His feet for refueling. Get to know God. Living His will is not a matter of weeks, months or even years – it's a life-long commitment.

Dr. Martin Luther has penned a song, *A Mighty Fortress Is Our God* in which he states:

> "And tho this world, with devils filled,
> Should threaten to undo us,
> We will not fear, for God hath willed
> His truth to triumph thru us.
> The prince of darkness grim,
> We tremble not for him—
> His rage we can endure,
> For lo, his doom is sure:
> One little word shall fell him.
> That word above all earthly pow'rs,
> No thanks to them abideth;
> The Spirit and the gifts are ours
> Thru Him who with us sideth.
> Let goods and kindred go,
> This mortal life also—
> The body they may kill
> God's truth abideth still;
> His kingdom is forever.

Yes, Luther was right on when he said "One little word shall fell him." Your deliverance is guaranteed when you have the name of Jesus on your lips. No demon can penetrate through His blood. Use it against any attack and you shall remain free. Conviction comes from the Holy Spirit. Condemnation comes from Satan. Maintain a strong daily prayer life. Know your weapons and know how to use them. Come near to God and he will come near to you. Take hold of Jesus and hold on for dear life. Your life may depend upon it.

Even The Old Testament Helps Us Out

We no longer have to fight our own battles. In 2 Chronicles 16:9 we read that "The eyes of the Lord range throughout the earth to strengthen those whose hearts are fully committed to him." If we are committed to the Lord He will give us strength when we are in need.

One of the strongest Old Testament verses is located in Habakkuk 3:19 of the *Amplified Bible*, "The Lord God is my strength, my personal bravery, and my invincible army; He makes my feet like hinds' feet and will make me to walk [not to stand still in terror, but to walk] and make [spiritual] progress upon my high places [of trouble, suffering, or responsibility]." We can only move ahead with the Lord. This Scripture certainly brings out that promise.

Exodus 14:14 in the *KJV* gives us the assurance that, "The Lord shall fight for you, and ye shall hold your peace." Deuteronomy 3:22 says that we should not fear: "Do not be afraid of them; the Lord your God himself will fight for you." Deuteronomy 20:4 promises us that "The Lord your God is the one who goes with you to fight for you against your enemies to give you victory."

For Further Study - Living A Victorious Life As Proclaimed In Psalms And Proverbs

The following verses are not written out with the hope that you will study the context of each and determine how each fits into your life.

Pray: Prov. 15:29 and Ps. 120:6; 141:2
Study the Word, believe and keep it: Prov. 4:13; 13:13; 30:5 and Ps. 119:105
Develop and keep a positive testimony: Prov. 25:11 and Ps. 128:1-2

Keep Satan at bay: Ps. 139:23-24

Forgive and repent: Ps. 86.5; 103:12; 139:23-24

Keep a positive attitude (sing unto the Lord): Ps. 89:1

Squelch gossip and don't speak negatively about other people: Prov. 18:21

Spread love and help others in need: Prov. 10:12

Use your talents for the Lord's work: Ps. 81:10

Live a righteous life according to the Word: Prov. 29:18; 30:5 and Ps. 4:3

Be a prayer warrior: Ps. 89:1

Be teachable: Prov. 8:33; 23:12

Know that you are blessed: Ps. 89:15-16

Be soft hearted, gentle, humble: Prov. 15:1-3, 33; 16:18, 32; and Ps. 51:17

Pray for wisdom and knowledge: Prov. 2:1-11; 3:13; 4:7; 17:27; Ps. 90:12

Live in peace: Ps. 29:11; 31:3; 34:4, 7-9; 50:15; 112:7

Know you're going to heaven: Ps. 13:5; 16:11; 27:1; 49:15; 116:15

Praise the Lord: Ps. 34:1; 47:1, 6-7; 66:1-2; 95:1-2; 96:1-2

Bless the Lord: Ps. 63: 3-4; 66:8; 103:1-2; 134:2

Place you trust and faith in the Lord: Ps. 5:11-12; 8:9-10; 37:4-5; 51:17; 55:16; 56:11; 61:8; 91:1-2

For Additional Further Study - Selected Spiritual Warfare Scriptures

Old Testament:
- Exodus 14:14
- Deuteronomy 31:6
- Joshua 1:8
- 1 Samuel 16:23
- 2 Chronicles 16:9a, 20:15b
- Psalm 23, 27, 34:4, 7, 22; 37; 91; 125:2
- Isaiah 54:17
- Nahum 1:7
- Habakkuk 3:19

- Zechariah 3:2

New Testament:
- Matthew 4:4, 7, 10; 12:29, 43-45, 48-50; 16:19, 23; 22:37; 26:41
- Mark 3:27; 9:29; 16:17
- Luke 1:37; 8:19-21; 10:19-20
- Acts 17:11
- 2 Corinthians 2:11; 5:17; 12:7-9
- Ephesians 4:27; 5:11; 6:10-18
- Philippians 4:13
- 1 Thessalonians 5:17
- Hebrews 4:12
- James 4:7
- 1 John 1:7; 4:1,4
- Jude
- Revelation 3:16; 12:11

These Scriptures are just some of the verses that can help begin your walk in your deliverance. Read them, study them, apply them. It's a daily battle, but remember that God is on our side and Satan is a defeated foe. God permits him to practice guerrilla warfare but his tactics are known so we must remember to use the strongest name in heaven and earth against him – *Jesus*!

Pastor Franklin Hunt Has Good Advice

Pastor Franklin Hunt from Fayetteville, NC has four steps to begin your walk in deliverance:

(1) "Face it. Do not deny your feeling s and don't blame others for your negative emotions. Face it as a man or woman who loves God. You will never change what you permit and never face what you deny."

(2) "Trace it. Get to the root of your conflict . Was it pride on your part? Did you reject godly advice? Was it the enemy attempting to create a rift. Did you misunderstand someone's comment? Identify the root and deal with that instead of the surface circumstances."

(3) "Erase it. By asking forgiveness, and at times facing the person directly to ask their forgiveness, you are erasing the offense. God will also blot it from any record in heaven and will cleanse it out of your spirit. The enemy may attempt to bring back a memory for a season, but the Holy Spirit will raise up and remind you that you need not remember a sin that God has forgotten."

(4) "Replace it. Old images can be replaced with new pictures. Make fresh memories. Build new relationships. Get on with your life as you leave your past behind."

Pastor Hunt has garnered much insight into the area of spiritual warfare and deliverance. His advice should be memorized, internalized and practiced. This certainly will help you overcome and conquer.

CHAPTER THIRTEEN

Getting Involved In Satanism And What Happens

Experimenting With Satanism

It is not uncommon for some youth to experiment with satanism. The experiment ends quickly for soon they are caught up in the occult and can find no way out – with the exception at times of severe physical abuse or even death. Often they are thrown into a dark hole with body parts, live rats and other items to destroy their minds. This is known as the "black hole experience." Sometimes coffins are used. When they are removed they now give their complete allegiance to the warlock or coven leader and are at his or her mercy. They probably now will be part of a coven or circle.

If the parents are in satanism often times young girls at the age of six or seven are used as an altar and must have sex with all the males in the group. The women and girls even perform a regular marriage ceremony to Satan and become his "bride." There are certain signs to look for if you feel your child or his or her cohorts and friends might be involved. In no way does the following list constitute satanic involvement if only a few of the items are present, but look for a combination or pattern of them which could possible give evidence of experimentation or involvement. Here is where you need to keep a close and careful watch over a sibling. Some aspects are:

(1) Possesses the *Satanic Bible, Book of Shadows, Buckland's Complete Book of Witchcraft, Shadows of the Supernatural*, etc. Many of these and others are available on the shelves of local bookstores.

(2) Possesses stolen Christian items as a chalice. This is used to mix blood and urine for communion to Satan. Recently I was called to a church that experienced a break-in with satanic symbols scrawled about the door and sidewalk. The first thing I asked the minister if the chalice was missing.

(3) Becomes an isolationist and withdraws from family but retains only a few friends whom he or she does not speak about. They do not have any Christian values but may go to church to hear about Satan and even read the *Bible* to find out more about him – thus misleading the parents who are unaware of their underlying reasons for their involvement in these false "Christian" activities.

(4) Develops rapid changes in personality, often experiencing deep seated depression.

(5) Kills small animals to use as a sacrifice to Satan.

(6) Possesses satanic jewelry (upside-down cross, goat's head, etc.).

(7) Draws satanic symbols but will not explain them to parents. When writing, he may use the Hobbit language. There are twenty-six letters in the Hobbit alphabet to match the English alphabet plus five sound combinations. A teacher called me to her school one day to decipher some strange writing along with a very large satanic symbol, the pentagram. In Hobbit language, it reads, "Satan Rules, Satan's under-ground for those who want to explore it, this is Satan's cross for those who wish to kill the b------ which one cannot stand;" "600 60 6;" "war against God's servants." The goat head (baphomet) was also drawn. This teacher then realized she was dealing with other students who also were caught up in the occult.

(8) Has an inordinate desire to play with the quiji board, Dungeons and Dragons and other satanic influenced games.

(9) Has an obsession with black clothing.

(10) Has an obsession with horror movies and reads books with themes as death, suicide, murder, blood, torture and other dark subjects.

(11) Exhibits physical cuts on wrists and other body parts along with occult tattoos.

(12) Does not use his real name but takes them from the *Satanic Bible* which lists fifty-one "Infernal Names."

(13) Uses the *Satanic Bible* to give "Invocation to Satan" and recites or reads the nineteen "Keys," performs satanic magic and rituals and memorizes the "Nine Satanic Statements," etc. This so-called "bible" is full of evil and ways of bringing destruction to your enemy and other damming statements that can lead someone astray.

(14) Despises the law, parents, teachers and anyone in authority. In school, his or her grades are failing.

(15) Becomes obsessed with certain heavy metal music by listening to radio, CD's or goes to their concerts. Many of these activities are beyond the understanding or knowledge of the parents.

(16) Enjoys spending time in cemeteries and "talking" with their "friends" who are dead.

(17) May have black lips and painted black finger-tips. If not painted, they may bruise nails by pounding them with a hammer.

(18) Has fears, nightmares, awakens screaming and sees visions of terror and death. They become so disturbed that no longer can they control their thoughts and actions.

(19) Holds secretive meetings with friends in basements, old churches no longer in use, out buildings and other locations as where not to draw attention.

Often parents are oblivious to what's happening and may refuse to believe that their child can be wrapped up in such evil, so either they do nothing or try to get help from sources who are not aware of such situations themselves.

Deliverance is difficult when this deep evil is so ingrained in a person, for often he or she does not want to be delivered. Here, someone familiar with demons and deliverance might be contacted but always remember, when the name of Jesus is invoked, the demons have to come out – and that is the only way a person can be set free.

Buckland's Complete Book of Witchcraft lists ways of becoming involved in the use of spells and charms, tarot cards, rituals, channeling and other Magik (magic) too numerous to mention in this book. The 1990 edition includes 251 pages including how to become a witch or warlock. If a youth has this book just think how he or she could influence their friends who also might want to "dabble" in its contents. The problem is that dabbling may lead to total involvement. Peer pressure plays a large part here. To be part of the gang, some youth will delve into most anything.

A Mother's Story

One day a mother called me who had a son in satanism. This is what she said that took place: they placed him in a snake pit (black hole experience) and sexually molested him. He was tied upside down in a tree and saw demons materialize. His mother said that when she tries to take him into church he claws, fights, screams, kicks and speaks to her in a different voice. She has no control over him and he hangs out with a "strange" group of friends. Out of her dilemma she cried out, as other mothers in the same situation, "What can I do?"

Getting Out Is Not Easy

One teen-aged girl who was involved in this dark realm told me every time she looks into a mirror she sees a green, grotesque entity with long straight black hair and with blood running out of its mouth. She said she constantly has nightmares but is afraid to leave her group because of the fear of death.

One day a women called me who wanted to get out of satanism but feared for her life. I told her to meet me at a certain location where I would take her to a "safe-house." From there, for her safety, she would be sent to other "safe-houses" throughout the United States for a period of two years. Her name and identity were changed and she had no contact with anyone in the past. Her protectors felt that after this period of time it would be safe for her to return home.

I have found that even when these people get out of satanism they still have problems from the past, so it is easy to get into it but extremely difficult to get out. When youth finally open up they will tell you that they have night-mares, see demonic beings and faces and hear strange voices. They are afraid to, or cannot talk about it. Some think about suicide and if someone does not get to them in time they may do it. Be there for them. They need to know that there is a way out - it's only through Jesus Christ. No matter how hard you feel the pull of Satan, remember that Jesus' pull is stronger.

According to the Satanic Ritual Calendar there are eighteen groupings of days for their celebrations starting from January 7, (St. Winebald Day) which requires an animal or human sacrifice. If it is a person, it must be a male between the ages of fifteen to thirty-three. They have eight Feast Days of oral, anal or vaginal sex. Halloween is the time for sex with the demons.

March 1, (St. Eichatadt Day) is the time of "drinking of human blood for strength and homage to the demons." There are others but I'm sure the reader will get a good idea of some of their activities. If someone tries to get out of satanism he or she might be the next sacrifice. The most significant of their Sabbats in order are: Halloween, May Eve, Summer Solstice and Winter Solstice.

Michigan State Police Findings Regarding Occult Criminal Investigation

The Michigan State Police in East Lansing's homicide investigations have found the following on bodies: (1) missing body parts, (2) stab wounds and cuts,

(3) branding iron or burn marks, (4) wax drippings on the victim or the ground, (5) oils or incense found on the body, (6) human or animal feces consumed or found on the victim, (7) blood-letting and (8) urine, drugs, wine, potions, etc., found in the victim's stomach. Now you may see how difficult it is to get out of satanism. Parents, who are your children's friends?

The Michigan State Police have found persons involved in satanism commonly rob graves, removing entire bodies or specific body parts as the skull and bones which will be used in rituals. They also practice mutilations in both animal and human sacrifices which may involve the use of the heart, lungs, intestines, ears, eyes or tongues. The police say these people are difficult to track down because they do not leave signs that are traceable.

What People Do To Get Into Satanism

Generally, to become part of a coven is to say the Lord's Prayer backwards and the Catholic Missal backwards. (The Missal is a book containing readings, prayers and rubrics used for Mass). They must prove they have made an animal or human sacrifice. They also walk backwards and talk backwards, e.g., "nema" for amen, "live" for evil and "redrum" for murder.

The State of Colorado has traced some occult activity which includes group meetings on a Friday or Saturday night in abandon buildings preferably in abandoned churches or in the woods. Their activity is shrouded in secrecy making detection virtually impossible. Colorado information reveals that during their sacrifices of dogs, cats or goats they speak in "strange" languages. Most groups ranged from twelve to thirty people and may contain persons from all strata of society.

Alphabets

I have found in my research of "infernal" books that the Hobbit language is one of the dominant ones used to communicate, but also the Runic alphabet and the Theban alphabet (also called Honorian, which some books call the Malachim, although some say this is another language altogether) are sometimes used. Egyptian hieroglyphics is another used as a magikal (magical) alphabet. Pictish and other alphabets are used but are too detailed to under-take in this book. Witches usually use these to communicate.

Satan Also Operates In Homes

Deuteronomy 7:26 says, "Do not bring a detestable thing into your house or you, like it, will be set apart for destruction. Utterly abhor and detest it, for it is set apart for destruction." Idols, heathen artifacts and masks and anti-Christian memorabilia are a no-no in a Christian home. This also includes some heavy metal rock groups. On a personal note, a minister told me that he and his wife went out of town for the weekend leaving their two teen-age daughters in charge of the house. When the couple returned everything seemed to be in an uproar so they asked the girls what had happened. The girls told them that their friends loaned them some heavy metal and satanic rock CD's. The couple told them to return the items to their friends, after which things returned to normal once again in their home.

In another incident, a teacher called me to her home because she was experiencing poltergeist. Doors would slam, faucets turn on, objects moved in the house and the words "I got cha" would emanate throughout the house. As I was leaving the house, her little dog ran to a cabinet. She spanked it but then it did the very same thing. I asked what she had in the cabinet. She said only some CD's. I found that they were of satanic rock groups which I destroyed and she has had no problems since. Her dog knew more about demons than she did!

Isaiah 13:21of *The Living Bible* tells us what can happen, "The houses will be haunted by howling creatures. Ostriches will live there, and the demons will come there to dance." Sad when demons have greater joy in a home than the residents. Houses too need the Lord's deliverance before they become a den for demons. Take olive oil and anoint all the doors and with an open *Bible* go into every room and command any ungodly spirit to leave; then dedicate each room to Jesus. This also stops poltergeist.

Sheri's Experience

One day a practicing attorney came over to our home. He said he was having problems and would like some help. We took him into our back yard gazebo where he told Sheri that he was having sex with a witch and that she had put curses on him. He stated that God had talked to him and appeared as a lizard, telling him that He wanted him to learn the difference between good and evil. Sheri mentioned to him that God would have other means of teaching him good vs evil and would not turn into a lizard. He reached out and touched Sheri's arm indicating to her that this was how it felt because his experience was so real. Immediately a red stripe appeared down her entire arm. She became very ill and immediately went into the house.

A few days later he appeared at our front door with his car in the driveway. He rang the door-bell; Sheri went to the door and identified him as the one we ministered to in our gazebo. No words were spoken but he just stared at her. She came into a room to get me and immediately went back to the door. Both he and the car were gone! Sheri ran out to the road but there were no cars in either direction. What is your interpretation of this story?

A Rude Awakening

One of my cousins lives in the Upper Peninsula of Michigan. I gave a presentation on satanism in one of the churches there. My cousin is a woodsman who takes people on hunting expeditions, fishing trips, etc. He said that he could take me to places where the satanists do their sacrificing. He stated that he has to be careful, for if he gets too close to such an area, he could get a knife in his chest from some of the traps that they lay.

Also, he stated that there are three rings of guards around an area. If you accidently walk too closely, the first guard would tell you to leave; if you continue, the second guard is much more firm and commands that you leave; if you do not heed his warning the third guard will take you in and you may never be heard from again. Of course I have not experienced this behavior but I take his word for it since his life is spent in the woods and he has much knowledge of all aspects of what happens in those heavily wooded areas.

Satanism is not to be taken lightly as these examples depict. Getting in may mean no way out! Do not be oblivious to the evidence of satanism out there. It is real and it is growing. Be observant – and be careful.

A Place To Turn – Hospital Help

After digging through my files from way back, I discovered an interesting article titled "Hospital unit specializes in Satanism" from the *Tribune-Star* (Terre Haute, IN), September 7, 1989 which I would like to share with you through quotes and paraphrase.

At Hartgrove Hospital in Chicago, "…they are creating one of the nation's first treatment programs to wean teen-agers from Satanism. I don't think there is any doubt Satanism is a growing problem. We don't know the percentages because so much is secretive, but we do know it is beginning to show up throughout the country." They have stated that there are not enough places to take the youth. The program primarily admits youth with behavioral and emotional problems where they spend four to six weeks in group counseling.

The personnel consist of specially trained psychiatrists, psychologists, social workers and nurses. "Youngsters involved in Satanism often exhibit unusual behavior which can include suicide attempts, drug use, sexual promiscuity, a drastic drop in grades, intensified rebellion, a strong interest in heavy metal music, role-playing games or horror films and the use of occult symbols such as '666' or upside-down crosses. They usually are intelligent, creative and bored with traditional pursuits. They generally have a feeling of being different and not belonging, and often are underachievers and generally have a feeling of being powerless."

The facility initially will take six patients at a time. This program seeks to undermine satanism's belief program which hampers conventional treatment. Since this was a new program, most likely they will be taking additional numbers of youth in for treatment. It is good news that finally the medical profession realizes that these involved youth need counseling, treatment and a place for them to turn.

CHAPTER FOURTEEN

Final Comments And Conclusion

What Demons Are Not

(1) ghosts – there is not such a thing. If people think they see a ghost it is really a demon.

(2) the spirits of dead people. One lady told me the seven apparitions floating around in her house are the souls of the "restless dead." The Book of Ecclesiastes states that the "dead know nothing" and have "no further place on the earth."

(3) the result of the OT union between "the sons of God and the sons of men," referring to the offspring of fallen angels and human women.

Why Study About The Enemy

I tell my congregations and youth groups not to be an authority on cults or the occult but be an authority on the *Bible*. If so, you can refute any false doctrines and false religions, but also you need to know the tactics of the enemy, for although Jesus defeated Satan and his minions at the cross, God allows him to practice guerrilla warfare.

Why We Should Know Satan's Devices

The *Amplified Bible* makes this clear, for 2 Corinthians 2:11 says, "To keep Satan from getting the advantage over us; for we are not ignorant of his wiles and intentions;" and in the KJV we read, "Lest Satan should get an advantage of us: for we are not ignorant of his devices." Furthermore, if you are not familiar with how the demons work you may be in deep trouble for your mind is in the middle with God on one side and Satan on the other. To whom will you give it? Ephesians 4:27 warns us that we are not to give the devil a foothold and Matthew 4:10 says we are to worship the Lord your God only and not to serve any other thing or being.

Rebellion And Falling Away From God's Word

1 Samuel 15:23 gives us strict warning not to refute and go against God's Word, "For rebellion is as the sin of witchcraft, and stubbornness is as iniquity and idolatry;" and in 2 Corinthians 11:3-4 again we are warned by Paul when he says what can happen if we fall away. "But I am afraid that just as Eve was deceived by the serpent's cunning, your minds may somehow be led astray from your sincere and pure devotion to Christ. For if someone comes to you and preaches a Jesus other than the Jesus we preached, or if you receive a different spirit from the one you received, or a different gospel from the one you accepted, you put up with it easily enough."

Dr. Martin Luther's Response

Dr. Martin Luther was often very graphic in his description of the devil. Asked how he overcomes Satan, he replied, "Well, when he comes knocking upon the door of my heart and asks 'Who lives here?' the dear Lord goes to the door and says 'Martin Luther used to live here but he has moved out. Now I live here.' The devil seeing the nail-prints in His hands and His pierced side, takes flight immediately."

Dr. Cecil Todd On How To Take Care Of The Devil

A very inspiring preacher and teacher of the Word, Dr. Cecil Todd of Revival Fires Ministry in West Branson, MO has a wonderful message on "How to Whip the Devil and Keep Going for God!" I wish I could cite it in its entirety but I will do my best to paraphrase some of the major concepts. He says that we should commit the following to our lives: "Winners never quit and quitters never win!" That's how we defeat Satan with the help of Jesus. Satan attacks from all directions and "he will throw everything at you, including the kitchen sink!"

Dr. Todd also states that if you are a soul winner for Jesus, the Devil will try harder than ever to stop you. He will use everything and everyone that he can including friends (even Christian friends) and even your own family members. If he can destroy your faith and fellowship with Christ that is a game with him, but it's heaven or hell for us. Many people think that becoming a Christian ends your problems but as 2 Timothy 3:12 warns "All who will live godly in Christ Jesus will suffer persecution." I like Dr. Todd's statement that "The symbol of Christianity is a Cross – not a couch!" He says that Jesus can make "scrappers out of scraps" and "winners out of sinners."

He goes on to say that some people scoff at the idea of a personal devil, but he asks, "If there is not a Devil, who is behind all the lust, sin and selfishness that destroys people's lives today? Who is behind all the greed and corruption in high places? Who is behind all the cheap politics and the 'sell out' of our country to the godless and anti-Christian forces running wreckless in our world today? Who is behind all the bloody wars that have taken so many lives? Who is behind all the murder, rape, robberies, broken homes and broken hearts in the world today?"

"Who is behind all the jealousy and envy, malicious deeds, the gossiping and cutting tongues, the hurt feelings, the hatred and unforgiveness in people's hearts? There is but one answer …" "THE DEVIL! He is still rebelling against God and against everyone who has decided to follow His Son, Jesus Christ!" Well said Dr. Todd. Satan is the source of all evil and if we do not know how to combat him, we are in for some horrendous trouble.

Dr. Todd mentions that either life's trials and hardships will make you "bitter" or "better." It's your choice. "God can bring good out of every circumstance that comes against us, if we let Him." Satan will win a few battles but not the war. He sums up his message with four ways to whip Satan and keep going for God: "(1) you must resist the Devil, (2) you must stay close to God, (3) you must stay busy for God, and (4) you must trust God's strength and not your own." This is Dr. Todd's personal plan – and it should be one that we all incorporate into our own lives.

God's Promises From A To Z (author unknown)

Although things are not perfect

Because of trial or pain

Continue in thanksgiving

Do not begin to blame

Even when the times are hard

Fierce winds are bound to blow

God is forever able

Hold on to what you know

Imagine life without His love

Joy would cease to be

Keep thanking Him for all the things

Love imparts to thee

Move out of "camp complaining"

No weapon that is known

On earth can yield the power

Praise can do alone

Quit looking at the future

Redeem the time at hand

Start every day with worship

To thank is a command

Until we see Him coming
Victorious in the sky
We'll run the race with gratitude
Xalting God most high
Yes, there'll be good times and yes some will be bad, but
Zion waits in glory…where none are ever sad!

Final Comments

We are not human beings going through a temporary spiritual experience, but we are spiritual beings going through a temporary human experience. Remember, all of the water in the ocean cannot sink a ship – unless it gets inside. So often we allow holes in our ship where Satan can start to fill with water. It is not enough to continue to bail the water, for in the long run this is futile. Make sure your "patchwork" is permanent – sealed and covered with the blood of the Lamb. Now your ship will remain afloat. A ship is not built to remain in the harbor.

Take it out on the sea of life and use it to help others who are struggling to keep their crafts from sinking. Attach your ship to theirs and pull them to shore. Give them the lifeline that can only come from Jesus. He will reward you for your efforts in helping a wayward sailor make it safely into His harbor of eternal life.

The deliverance team and I pray that his book has been a blessing to you and has achieved the goals set forth throughout its contents. Remember not only be hearers of the Word but doers also. Hopefully, you now will be able to cope with spiritual warfare and remove Satan as the source of many of your secular and spiritual problems; also, that you can handle, with the help of Jesus, deliverance and the removal of demons from those who are overcome with their influence.

Final Poem And Scriptures To Highlight Your Day

I realize many of the examples in this book may be difficult to ascertain so I would like to leave you with some positive quotes which I feel are pertinent to close off this book. May you dwell on these and see the joy of the Lord in each. Always keep a positive attitude for the joy of the Lord is your strength.

This poem was sent to me by a former church member:

"Love is patient, love is kind,
Love is feelings, around the heart entwined.
Love understand, love is trust,
Love is forgiving, and that is a must.
Love is a heart that has eyes to see,
Love is a friend, who lets me be me."

Jeremiah 29:10-13 (*The Living Bible*) - "For I know the plans I have for you, says the Lord. They are plans for good and not for evil, to give you a future and a hope. In those days when you pray, I will listen. You will find me when you seek me, if you look for me in earnest."

2 Corinthians 6:11 (*TLB*) - "… I have told you all my feelings; I love you with all my heart."

Romans 13:12 - "The night is nearly over; the day is almost here. So let us put aside the deeds of darkness and put on the armor of light."

And finally, the Benediction of the Lord:

John 14:27 - "Peace I leave with you; my peace I give you. I do not give to you as the world gives. Do not let your hearts be troubled and do not be afraid."

Numbers 6:24-26 - "The Lord bless thee, and keep thee:
The Lord make his face shine upon thee, and be gracious unto thee:
The Lord lift up his countenance upon thee, and give thee peace."
Amen. So shall it be.

BIBLIOGRAPHY

SCRIPTURES TAKEN FROM THE FOLLOWING BIBLES

Amplified Bible, The. Lockman Fdn. POB 2279, La Habra, CA. 90632. www. lockman.org. 1965.

Dake's Annotated Reference Bible. Dake Publishing, Inc. 764 Martins Chapel Rd. Lawrenceville, GA, 30045. www. info@dake.com. 1963.

Living Bible, The. Tyndale House Publishers. 351 Executive Dr. Carol Stream, IL 60188. www. tyndale.com. 1971.

NIV Study Bible, The. The Zondervan Publishing House. Grand Rapids, MI 49506. www. Zondervan.com. 1985.

OTHER CHRISTIAN REFERENCES

Hymnal For Worship & Celebration. "A Mighty Fortress is Our God" – (Martin Luther). Word Music. 1986.

Lion Handbook The History of Christianity, A. Dr. Tim Dowley (Editor). Lion Publishing. 1990.

Nelson's New Illustrated Bible Dictionary. Ronald F. Youngblood (General Editor). Thomas Nelson Publishers, 1995.

Zondervan Pictorial Bible Dictionary, The. Merrill C. Tenney (General Editor). Zondervan Publishing House. 1967.

GENERAL REFERENCE

Josephus. Flavius Josephus. Translated by William Whiston. Kregel Publications. 1960.

Tribune Star (Newspaper – Terre Haute, IN). Max Jones (Editor). September 7, 1989.

Webster's New World College Dictionary, 4th Edition. Michael Agnes (Editor in Chief), MacMillan USA. 1999.

REFERENCES FROM THE "DARK SIDE"

Buckland's Complete Book of Witchcraft. Raymond Buckland. Llewellyn Publications. 1990.

New Age Catalogue, The. Paul Zuromski (Editor and Publisher). Island Publishing Company. 1988.

Satanic Bible, The. Anton Szandor LaVey. Avon Books. 1969.

Shadows of the Supernatural. Colin Chapman. Lion Publishing. 1990.

INDIVIDUAL QUOTATION REFERENCES

Hunt, Pastor Dr. Franklin – Fayetteville, NC.

Thigpen, Dr. Paul – Contributing Editor to *Discipleship Journal* and staff editor for Prison Fellowship Ministries.

Todd, Pastor Dr. Cecil – Revival Fires Ministry, Branson West, MO.

Wilcox, Ella Wheeler, *Winds of Faith*.